I0053127

Operations Manual

by Jay Butler and Dr. Robert Hagopian

AssetProtectionServices.com

ISBN 978-0-9914644-3-2

OPERATIONS MANUAL

HOW TO USE YOUR CORP • LLC • LP • TRUST

Table of **Contents**

Disclaimer

The publication is copyrighted © 2016 by Asset Protection Services of America (hereinafter "APSA") with all rights reserved. No part of this publication may be reproduced, retransmitted or rebroadcast in any form or by any means without the express prior written consent of the copyright holder.

Information contained in this publication has been prepared for continuing research and, although these materials may be technical in nature, carries no weight other than being educational in purpose. The materials are provided only as a starting point in order for the reader to undertake his or her own investigation of the subject matter contained herein.

This publication has been garnered from sources deemed reliable at the time of rendering. Since laws, rules, rulings, regulations, statutes and codes are constantly changing and evolving, the information may not be current and APSA takes no responsibility for updating, omitting or correcting any information in this publication.

APSA offers no guarantees the information in this book as being comprehensive, exhaustive, accurate or complete and furthers the information provided is on an "AS IS" basis. Any guidance or reliance on the content found in this publication is at the sole risk of the user. APSA offers no assurances as to the suitability of any particular service or strategy meeting any stated aims, goals or objectives. APSA strongly recommends the reader seek independent accounting, financial, investing, legal, tax or other professional advice.

No representations or warranties are given or implied to render any accounting, financial, investing, legal, tax or other professional advice. No accounting, financial, investing, legal, tax or other professional advice is intended, approved or authorized by APSA. If any accounting, financial, investing, legal, tax or other professional advice is required, then a competent professional should be sought.

APSA and any APSA advisors, directors, employees, members, officers, partners, professional agencies, professional intermediaries, shareholders, staff, ultimate beneficial owners and any other affiliated firms or third-parties wherever situated, take no responsibility whatsoever, whether individually or collectively, for the manner in which the reader may choose to interpret or use the information presented in this publication. APSA shall not be held liable for any civil or criminal liability or damages whether direct, indirect, special or consequential resulting from any interpretations or use of the information provided in this publication.

This publication shall not be taken as sanctioning or advocating any unlawful act or for any improper use of any entity structure, asset protection, tax strategy or estate planning activity, nor for any illegal or fraudulent purposes.

Asset Protection Services of America

The inverted "V" displayed on our shield is the uppercase letter "L" in ancient Greek identifying the people of Lacedaemonia, which in historical times was the proper name for the Spartan state. The Greek cry "Molõn Labé" means "Come and Get Them" as spoken by King Leonidas in response to the Persian army's demand for the outnumbered Spartans (300 against 300,000) to surrender their weapons during battle in the narrow pass or 'hot gates' of Thermopylae in 480 B.C. The iconic expression has become a symbol of courage to defend that which belongs to you, even if faced against overwhelming or insurmountable odds.

Author

Jay Butler is the Managing Director of Asset Protection Services of America, the former Managing Director of Asset Protection Services International, Ltd and the former Vice-President of Sales and Marketing for Corporate Support Services of Nevada Inc. Mr. Butler holds a Bachelor's Degree of Fine Arts from Boston University.

Jay has provided customized business entity structuring for clients in all 50 states along with some of the most respected names in the industry including the Jay Mitton organization "the father of asset protection" and Real Estate Investor Association seminars.

While working with Wealth Protection Concepts, LLC under the tutelage of the former Las Vegas and North Las Vegas city attorney Carl E. Lovell Jr. (now deceased from Leukemia), Mr. Butler was bestowed the title of "Asset Protection Planner" for his competency and experience. He also co-authored the first edition of his book "Cover Your Assets: Legal Authorities on Asset Protection, Tax Strategies and Estate Planning" © 2006 with Dr. Lovell.

While residing in Switzerland, Mr. Butler was the Associate Director of "CO-Handelszentrum GmbH" providing Swiss company formation and administration services and executed a full-range of fiduciary responsibilities including sales, client support and international corporate compliance services (KYC, FATCA, AML, FATF and Swiss Code of Obligations).

Jay builds his relationships through consistent attention to detail and reliable support. He has traveled extensively throughout the United States (having visited 49 of the 50 states), explored 36 nations worldwide, and has lived in a total of 7 countries throughout North America, Central America, the Middle East, North Africa and Europe.

Dr Robert Hagopian is semi-retired and the former CEO of Nevada Trustee Services Group Inc, which has provided trustee services to attorneys and law firms throughout the United States since 2005, and the former CEO of the Commerce Bank Ltd in Hong Kong.

Since 1968, Robert has traveled extensively throughout Asia and lived in Japan, Hong Kong and the Philippines with current residency and offices in Manilla.

Dr. Hagopian holds a Bachelor of Science (BS) degree in business administration, an MsD (doctorate) in philosophy and a "jure Dignitatis" Bachelor of Laws degree.

Since 1984, Dr. Hagopian has been structuring business entities for optimum wealth preservation, profitability, asset protection and limiting personal liability through the use of domestic corporations, limited liability companies and various trust vehicles.

Robert has developed innovative processes for the acquisition, holding and marketing of real property. In 2008, Dr. Hagopian applied for the patent-pending "Equity Recovery Program". Based on IRC 351 rules for the transference of real estate to a corporation, the program lawfully avoids capital gains tax, self-employment and state taxes upon the sale of real property.

Contact Us

Please browse our website at www.AssetProtectionServices.com and contact us to schedule your free private asset protection consultation. We welcome the opportunity to hold a 3-way conference call with your tax advisor and/or legal counsel to address any specific questions or concerns you may have. Experience has demonstrated it favorable to have all related parties "on the same page" when creating your structure.

Asset Protection Services of America
701 South Carson Street (Suite #200)
Carson City, Nevada 89701-5239
Office   (775) 461-5255
Skype   Jay_Butler
E-Mail   info@AssetProtectionServices.com
Website   www.AssetProtectionServices.com

Books by Jay Butler and Dr. Robert Hagopian

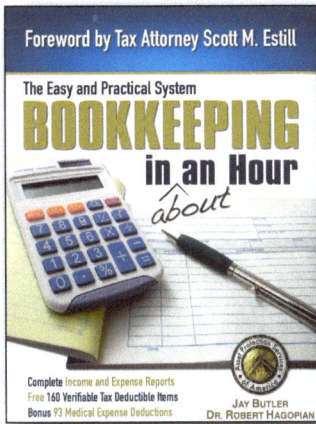

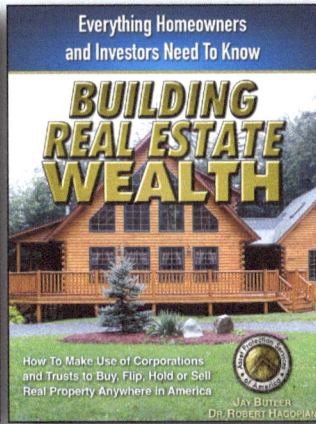

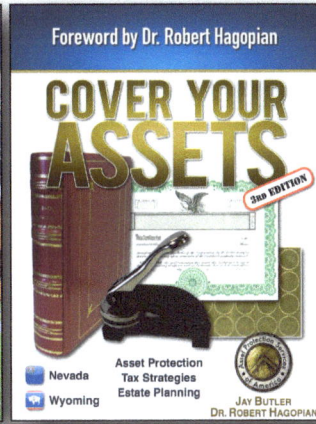

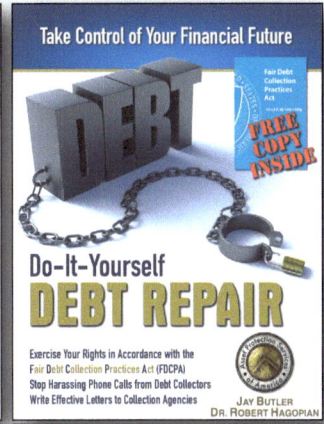

Bookkeeping in About an Hour — ISBN 978-0-9914644-0-1
Building Real Estate Wealth — ISBN 978-0-9914644-1-8
Cover Your Assets (*3rd Edition*) — ISBN 978-0-9914644-2-5
Do-It-Yourself Debt Repair — ISBN 978-0-9914644-7-0

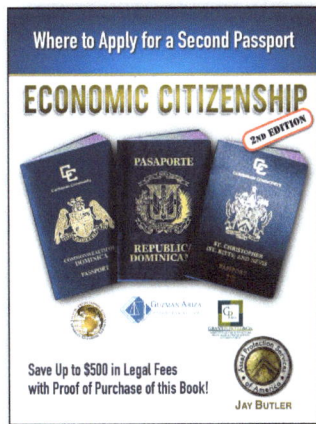

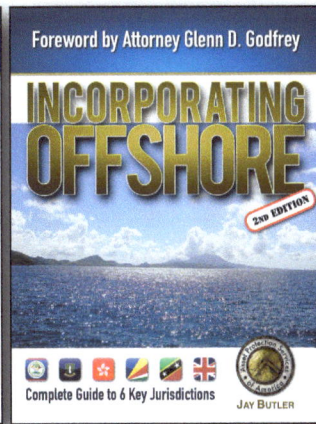

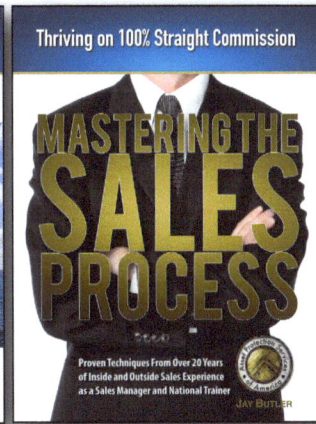

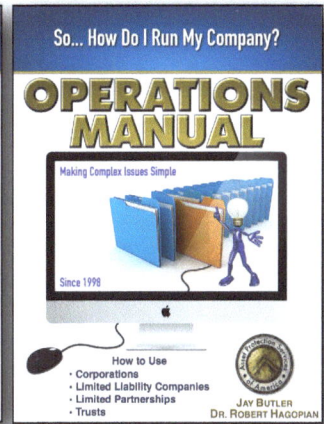

Economic Citizenship (*2nd Edition*) — ISBN 978-0-9914644-4-9
Incorporating Offshore (*2nd Edition*) — ISBN 978-0-9914644-5-6
Mastering the Sales Process — ISBN 978-0-9914644-6-3
Operations Manual — ISBN 978-0-9914644-3-2

**Business
Formalities**

Maintaining Business Documents

Maintaining complete and accurate documentation and carrying out the business formalities is imperative to protect the corporate shield from being broken. 'Business Formalities' are procedures of documentation that track the corporation's thought and activity process. More specifically, these formalities are in the form of corporate resolutions, amendments, notes, and meeting minutes of activities conducted. Assembling these forms within the corporate record book legitimizes the business conducted by validating their appropriateness, authenticity and authorization. ***Throughout this section, terms relating to 'corporate' or 'corporation' are (wherever possible) equally applicable to Limited Liability Companies and Limited Partnerships.***

To many, time spent keeping business records is unproductive time. However, the truth is that it is essential to properly maintaining your corporation. Are you prepared to stand personally liable for all of the debts of the Corporation that you assumed would be its debts and not yours or sacrifice tax benefits you planned upon receiving from your Corporation?

Where the individual loses planned for tax benefits or is held liable for the Corporation's debts, it is never the fault of the Corporation, rather, the blame lies with the corporate personnel, officers, directors and shareholders who do not maintain books and records proving that the Corporation had an existence separate and apart from its investors.

The downfall of the entrepreneur lacking proper corporate record keeping is that he or she can't prove that whatever was done was done on behalf of the Corporation and not for personal reasons. The very fact that the entrepreneur didn't keep records shows that he or she didn't respect the corporation's separate identity. And it hits where it hurts most in the pocketbook of the owners as well as in the corporation's cash drawer.

Without fail, you must uphold the responsibilities of keeping your corporate records book and and company records in compliance with all the laws and regulations. This 'Operations Manual' is intended to help you accomplish that goal.

Respecting the Corporate Identity

✔ Conducting Business in the Corporate Name

When doing business with third parties, the officers and directors must make it clear that they are acting on behalf of the corporation and not in their individual capacity. Correspondence should be sent out under the proper corporate letterhead and contracts should be entered into only with the corporation with you as a signatory. Unless the documents reflects a transaction is entered into on behalf of the corporation and all necessary agreements are entered into under the corporation's name, the corporate entity may not survive a challenge in a lawsuit.

✔ Bank Accounts

Corporate bank accounts and accounting records must be separate and distinct from the individual. A corporate bank account cannot be treated as if it were the account of an officer or director. Corporate income and assets must be separately accounted for on the books of the corporation. One of the biggest mistakes people make is to move money and property back and forth between yourself and your corporation without properly accounting for such movement in the records of the corporation. This is a fatal mistake, and under these circumstances, the court would likely disregard the corporate entity entirely.

For example if you are operating a Nevada corporation, even though you do not live in Nevada, it is best to establish a Nevada bank account to legitimize the presence of the corporation in Nevada. If for convenience, you want a bank account in your home state, there is no problem with that, but make sure that it is *in addition* to a Nevada bank account.

When using a home state bank account for your Nevada Corporation, it is necessary to make a deposit in Nevada first and then transfer money (via check), to your home state bank account. This is the cleanest way to end up with corporate funds in your home state to give you access to corporate cash. This process helps solidify your Nevada corporation as operating in Nevada and will reduce your home state tax burden as well because you can send only what is absolutely required in your home state.

All interest earned from a bank account is reported annually to the IRS. Therefore, if you desire to keep the IRS as far away as possible, set up a non-interest bearing checking account for the corporation.

✔ Bona Fide Presence

It is possible to have your case decided under Nevada law even though events transpired in another state if Nevada has a "substantial relationship to the parties" and it was so agreed in the disputed contract. The Nevada corporate presence can be achieved by employing our Nevada Address service from most incorporating companies.

✔ Does the Corporation Conduct Some Kind Of Business?

Compliance with these few points is the 'basics' to prove that your corporation is engaged in business and is a legitimate entity, separate and apart from you. It is important that anyone who comes in contact with the corporation know with whom they are dealing. Therefor your business cards, letterheads, invoices, statements and stationary identify your entity. Pay close attention to these important points as it will keep you out of trouble and on the path of savings and enable you to enjoy all the benefits and protections that a corporation offers.

Recording Corporate Thoughts and Actions

A entity can do everything you can do, except think. Its Board of Directors does its thinking for it. Therefore, when a corporation has 'thoughts', those thoughts must be expressed in written form and contained in the corporate records as proof that it was, in fact, the corporation that thought and acted. Each time a corporation makes a major, out-of-the-ordinary decision; it should be noted in the corporate records book in the form of minutes or resolutions. When that is done, the corporate entity is preserved and safe.

The fewer Stockholders that a corporation has, the more important this type of record keeping becomes especially in the case of a one-person corporation, were that single person is literally **everything**! You hear of outsiders penetrating the corporate veil. This event and problem is entirely blown out of proportion. Your corporate veil cannot and will not be penetrated if the corporate formalities are properly followed and there is no fraud or wrongful intent perpetrated. This is why it is all-important to observe corporate formalities. Courts look at corporate records to determine if the corporation has acted as a corporation or as an extension (or alter ego) of its owner.

The good news is that you don't need to document routine business decisions, only those that require formal board of director or shareholder approval. In other words, it's not required by law or practice that you clutter up your corporate records book with mundane business records about purchasing supplies or products, hiring or firing employees, deciding to launch new services or products or any of the host of other ongoing business decisions. But key legal, tax and financial decisions absolutely should be acted on by your board of directors, and occasionally by all of your shareholders.

'Key' Corporate Decisions

✓ The proceedings of annual meetings of directors and shareholders, the issuance of stock to new or existing shareholders.

✓ The purchase of real property

✓ The authorization of a significant loan amount or substantial line of credit.

✓ The making of important federal or state tax elections.

These, and other key decisions, should be made by your board of directors or shareholders and backed with corporate paperwork. That way, you'll have solid documentation in the event key decisions are questioned or reviewed later by corporate directors, shareholders, creditors, the courts or the IRS.

Having your board of directors ratify important corporate decisions doesn't necessarily mean dragging directors to a formal meeting, although this is one option. Corporate decisions can legally be made over the phone, by mail, fax machine, computer email or bulletin board conference, or any other practical means of communication among directors or shareholders. And once decisions are made, there are several easy-to-use ways to document these decisions -- by preparing written minutes for a corporate meeting or preparing written consent forms to be signed by the directors or shareholders. If the consent form method is used, no meeting is held; instead, directors sign a form that shows agreement to a particular transaction or decision.

Recording Corporate Decisions

Why should you bother to prepare minutes of meetings or written consents for important corporate decisions? For starters, annual corporate meetings are required under state law. If you fail to pay at least minimal attention to these ongoing legal formalities, you may lose the protection of your corporate status.

Your legal paperwork provides a record of important corporate transactions. This 'paper trail' can be important if disputes arise. You can use this paper trail to show your directors, shareholders, creditors, suppliers, the IRS and the courts that you acted appropriately and in compliance with applicable laws, regulations or other legal requirements. Formally documenting key corporate actions is a good way of keeping shareholders informed of major corporate decisions.

Directors of small corporations commonly approve business transactions in which they have a material financial interest. Your minutes or consent forms can help prevent legal problems by proving that these self-interested decisions were arrived at fairly, after full disclosure to the board and shareholders.

Banks, trusts, escrow and title companies, property management companies and other institutions often ask corporations to submit a copy of a board or shareholder resolution approving the transaction that is being undertaken, such as a loan, an authorized signatory, purchase or rental of property.

Three Methods to Document Formal Decisions

There are three basic ways to make and document formal corporate decisions made by a corporation's board of directors or shareholders.

✓ **Real Meeting With Minutes**

Your directors or shareholders and all interested parties get together in a real meeting and discuss and vote on items of corporate business. During or after the meeting, written minutes are prepared showing the date, time, place and purpose of the meeting and the decisions (resolutions) approved by the board of directors or shareholders.

✓ **Paper Meeting With Minutes**

Under this procedure, the directors or shareholders informally agree to a specific corporate action or actions, such as the election of new directors. Then minutes are prepared as though the decision were approved at a real meeting of directors or shareholders. We call meetings of this sort "paper" meetings, since the meeting takes place on paper only.

A paper meeting is often used by corporations that do not want to go to the trouble of holding a real meeting, but do want to maintain a corporate records history, complete with traditional formal minutes. While not specifically sanctioned under corporate statutes, a paper meeting with minutes is a common form of corporate documentation. It should present no problems as long as the decisions reflected in the minutes of the paper meeting represent actual decisions reached by your board or shareholders. This procedure is quite similar to taking action by written consent, discussed below, with one key difference: Formal minutes are prepared when a paper meeting is held.

✓ **Action by Written Consent**

This is the quickest and least formal way of taking formal corporate action. The directors or shareholders consent to a decision or action in writing by signing a written consent form. Minutes for a real or "paper" meeting are not prepared. Only the written consent forms are kept in the corporate records book, to indicate that directors and shareholders made necessary decisions.

When to Use Resolutions

You will find that, for your own corporate protection and security, you may want to have a lot of paperwork in your corporate record books. It is a good idea to document all that you wish to accomplish and all that you have accomplished. Sometimes you may find it pays to wait until the end of the year, to reconstruct some things and see what it is that you want in those records to cover you if anyone comes in to verify your records.

The role of the Secretary is to create 'corporate resolutions' which are a simple and effective means to record corporate and managerial activities. With a corporate resolution, a physical meeting does not have to actually take place. Corporate resolutions are the easiest way to manage and document a corporation's actions as opposed to someone taking notes and typing out an entire meeting that has taken place. Just state the specifics of what you are trying to accomplish. Both directors and stockholders can handle corporate affairs through resolutions, but generally it is the directors that hold the meetings that decide changes or significant business of a corporation.

One thing to keep in mind with your corporate resolutions or meeting minutes is that they can be created after the fact. It is a simple practice of creating corporate resolutions once something has occurred. This way you know why it was created, exactly who did it, when it happened, and what actually occurred. Then you can go back and create the necessary paperwork that describes the approval of such activity taking place. Postdate these resolutions as long as something did take place. In a legal situation, corporations that did not properly keep good records all of the time suddenly find that their corporations are full of records just in the nick of time.

Resolutions don't have to be as formally written as we have put them together, but you want to be sure that your focus is clear and concise so as not to confuse anyone who may read it. The attorneys have put their language, often referred to as 'legalese', into far too many things and only seem to confuse most people, which I sometimes think was its intent.

Questions and Answers

Question   **How do I best choose a method for documenting corporate decisions?**

Answer   Each of the three ways of reaching and documenting formal corporate decisions has its own advantages. You'll simply need to settle on the approaches that best suit your corporation's needs and the temperament of its directors and shareholders.

Real Meetings	allow the participants to meet face to face and arrive at decisions that require the give-and take of conversation, argument or persuasion engaged in by participants.
Paper Meetings	like real meeting, also results in the preparation of formal minutes that document board or shareholder decisions, but does not require the time and effort involved in getting everyone together in a meeting.
Written Consent	procedures allow the quickest and simplest of all, allowing the board or shareholders to agree to an uncontested item of business with a minimum of formality and paperwork.

Sometimes it will be clear that you really do need to hold a formal meeting. In other situations, it would be a waste of time to do so. Sometimes, any one or two, or even all three, approaches will serve you well. In other words, you can utilize whichever method works best under the circumstances.

Question   **Why bother to document corporate decisions?**

Answer   Corporate minutes and consent forms serve a dual role: They not only show that important corporate decisions were reached with the proper notice and vote of your directors or shareholders; they also allow you to set out the reasons for these decisions. This can be crucial later if a corporate decision is examined by the IRS as part of a tax audit or scrutinized by a court as evidence in a lawsuit. In other words: One of the main reasons for preparing minutes is to document and substantiate important corporate decisions.

Likewise, your minutes may be used to document corporate strategies and decisions to incur expenses that might later be the subject of controversy or even lawsuits. Examples include the settling of a claim against a disgruntled employee or shareholder or the decision to implement safeguards in a hazardous location or line of corporate activity (for example, paying for protective measures for pedestrians at a construction site or implementing manufacturing controls in producing a consumer product).

Another simple reason to prepare regular minutes, even if your directors don't need to meet to reach a decision, is that it looks good. If, for example, you later sell your business, a formal record keeping system can serve you well. Also, minutes can be important, in and of themselves, to show that you are entitled to the benefits that arise from, the separate legal and tax status of your corporation.

Example   The IRS audits your closely held corporation and requests copies of minutes of all annual and special meetings of your corporation. If your corporate record book is bare, or contains minutes for just a few meetings over the life of your corporation, the IRS will be less inclined to see your side of any tax disputes that may arise during the course of the audit (such as the reasonableness of salaries or bonuses paid to the shareholder-employees of your small corporation).

Also realize that you risk losing the benefit of a corporate structure if you don't comply with paperwork required of corporations. For instance, a court may decide to disregard the corporate entity and hold the shareholders personally liable for claims against the corporation if people running the business have not undertaken standard corporate formalities and procedures, such as holding and documenting meetings, issuing stock (not required in Nevada) and keeping corporate funds separate from personal funds.

Question   **What paperwork should a corporation prepare?**

Answer   At a minimum, prepare written minutes (either for real or paper meetings) for all annual meetings scheduled in your bylaws. Typically, this means preparing minutes for an annual shareholders' meeting followed by minutes for an annual directors' meeting.

Also prepare formal corporate documentation for all-important legal, tax, financial or business decisions reached by the directors or shareholders during the year. This documentation can be in the form of minutes for a special meeting - again, either real or on paper - or written consent forms signed by your directors or shareholders.
By preparing this simple paperwork, you will have prepared a paper trail of important corporate decisions, which should give your corporate records book enough "girth" to help satisfy the courts, IRS and others that you attended to provide the necessary legal and tax necessities.

Question   **When can written consents be safely used?**

Answer   Legally, written consents work just as well as written minutes of meetings to document director or shareholder decisions. Moreover, they are the quickest way to approve and document a formal decision by the corporation's board or shareholders since they do not require time and effort to hold a meeting and prepare minutes. Directors or shareholders simply sign a consent form that states the action or business approved. The written consent form is then placed in the corporate records book as proof of the decision.

Depending on the situation you may decide to use written consents, but you should do so after careful consideration of the potential weakness inherent in written consents. If a number of directors or shareholders are involved (when they do not directly work in the business), a request to sign a written consent form may come as a surprise to an outside director or shareholder.

Many corporations decide that a real meeting works best to let outsiders in on the reasons for important corporate decisions. The IRS and the courts usually expect to see written minutes, at least for basic corporate formalities such as the annual directors and shareholders meetings. Most corporations decide that written minutes look better, and are more appropriate, to document the proceedings of annual directors and shareholders meetings, even if a real meeting is not necessary because decisions are routine and all shareholders and directors agree to the proposed decision. All this being said, however, there is still a role for the written consent procedure in some circumstances:

One-Person Corporations   Written consent forms are particularly useful in one-person corporations where one individual owns and manages the corporation as its only shareholder and director. The consent form procedure allows the sole corporate director-shareholder to formally approve corporate decisions without going to the trouble of preparing minutes for a pretend meeting. The same holds true for corporations where two people who work closely are the only shareholders of a corporation.

Non-Controversial Decisions   Where time is not of the essence and where a face-to-face meeting of directors or shareholders is not necessary, it may make sense to take action by written consent. There shouldn't be a problem as long as minutes are kept for annual meetings and meetings where important decisions are discussed.

Question   **What's the best way to hold meetings for closely held corporations?**

Answer   Most closely held corporations have only a few shareholders and directors. In closely held corporations, annual meetings of directors and shareholders are held mostly as a formality. At the annual shareholders' meeting, the current board of directors is usually elected, en masse, to a new term (usually one year). At the annual directors' meeting, each current director routinely accepts office for the upcoming year.

Unless the election, or re-election, of a director is contested or an important item of business needs to be raised at an annual shareholders or directors' meeting, many small corporations may dispense with holding real annual meetings. Instead, the secretary of the corporation prepares minutes for a paper meeting showing the election of the board plus any other business the shareholders and directors agree upon in advance.

Question   **How to hold corporate meetings with inactive directors or shareholders?**

Answer   Corporations with at least one director or shareholder who doesn't work actively in the business often find it's best to hold annual and special meetings in person. Even if the business conducted is routine, this gives the outsiders a chance to ask questions before voting on the decision at hand.

Holding an in-person meeting is particularly important for annual shareholders' meetings. Even if the election of the board is a formality, holding an annual shareholders' meeting allows outside shareholders a chance to catch up on corporate business and leave the meeting satisfied that their capital investment in the corporation is in safe, capable hands. In other words, an annual shareholders' meeting can serve the same purpose as the annual report sent to shareholders in large, publicly held corporations.

Question   **Is it necessary to hold / prepare minutes and resolutions for all decisions?**

Answer   No. People who work at incorporated businesses hold many scheduled and impromptu (ad hoc) meetings throughout the year to discuss and resolve items of ongoing business. In a small corporation, the directors and shareholders who also work for the corporation are likely to be in attendance in their capacity as regular corporate employees without donning their director or shareholder hats.

Normally, you do not need to prepare corporate minutes or consents to document a garden-variety business or staff meeting. However, if what starts out as a routine matter of corporate business discussed at an informal meeting takes on important legal or tax overtones, you should record those decisions by preparing corporate minutes or consents. (*See below, for a list of the types of decisions customarily made at formal directors' meetings and shareholders' meetings*.)

Question   **What decisions should the board of directors make?**

Answer   The bulk of a corporation's formal decision making is made by the board of directors. The board of directors should approve important legal, tax and financial matters or those affecting the overall management of the corporation. Typical director decisions reached at corporate meetings or agreed to by written consent include the following:
- Setting officer and key employee salary amounts and fringe benefits;
- Amending corporate articles of incorporation or bylaws (article amendments must usually be ratified by shareholders);
- Declaring dividends;
- Authorizing the issuance of additional shares of stock;
- Purchasing insurance;
- Approving real estate construction, lease, purchase or sale;
- Appointing key corporate officers and departmental managers;
- Approving the terms of the loan of money to or from shareholders, directors, officers and banks or other outsiders.

Question   **What decisions are made (or ratified) by shareholders?**

Answer   Corporate shareholders should meet annually, typically to elect the board of directors to another term of office. If the board of directors serves for longer than one-year terms, or if the board is divided (classified) into groups, the shareholders may meet less frequently to elect the board. Or they may only elect a portion of the board at each annual shareholder meeting.

Shareholders are asked to participate in other corporate decisions less frequently than the board. These special shareholder decisions usually consist of structural changes to the corporation or decisions that affect the stock rights or values of the shareholders.

Bylaws typically set forth the major corporate decisions that shareholders are required under state law to participate in, either by ratifying (approving) a previously reached board decision or by making a decision independent from the board. Typical shareholder decisions include the following:
- Electing the board of directors;
- Ratifying amendments to articles;
- Approving changes in the rights, privileges or preferences of shares issued by the corporation;
- Approving the sale of substantial corporate assets;
- Agreeing to dissolve the corporation.

Question   **What happens if directors and shareholders are the same person?**

Answer   In small, closely held corporations, the shareholders and directors are very often one and the same. Obtaining shareholders' approval is really the same as obtaining directors' approval, except the directors must put on their shareholder hats prior to attending a shareholder meeting or signing a shareholder consent form. In these situations, it's common to schedule the directors' and shareholders' meetings one after the other on the same day, or pass out both directors' and shareholders' written consent forms to each director-shareholder at the same time.

Question   **What legal formalities are required for a corporation to be a legal entity?**

Answer   If an entity is to be treated and recognized as a corporation, it must look and act like a corporation and observe the corporate formalities. Here are some generally accepted additional rules to follow in order not to get "trapped" into being classified as not being a "legal corporation".

Hold Required Meetings   Annual meetings are required of the Stockholders and Directors. These must be properly recorded in the corporation record book. Under Nevada law these meetings can be held anywhere at any time, within or out of the state. Other state laws differ from state to state. If you are incorporated in any other state, check the corporation code in your state.

Create Resolutions   Aside from the required annual meetings, the easiest way to govern and observe corporate formalities is by resolutions. These are much simpler and faster to prepare than minutes of a meeting. Put lots of resolutions in your corporate record book concerning everything you do, and you will be protecting the corporation.

Observe Articles & Bylaws The Corporate bylaws set out the specific structure of the corporation. They are created and adopted by the Board of Directors of the corporation. They set forth the procedure and operations for the corporation and the roles and responsibilities of each officer, director and shareholder within the corporation.

Any specific boundaries that you wish the corporation to be bound by can be set forth in the corporate bylaws. The bylaws give the corporation an operating framework to work within. Any matters not specifically adopted in the bylaws of the corporation should be set forth in a corporate resolution and approved meeting minutes.

Never Commingle Funds Never commingle your personal funds or expenditures with those of the corporation. The corporation MUST have its own separate bank account and you should have your own personal bank account; do not pay personal expenses out of the corporate checking account. For instance, you do not write a corporate check for groceries or simply for cash without any explanation as to where the cash went. Keep your accounts clean.

Also, for tax reasons, it is vital to put adequate explanations on the corporate checks you write and to have receipts or cash receipts to back them up. For example, in the case of a company car, the corporation pays all the expenses, but the checks must be made out so that this is readily ascertainable.

You as an individual may accumulate, for example, cash receipts for gasoline, oil changes and so on. When the Corporation writes you a check for those items, the check should be identified as "***Reimbursement***" which must be itemized.

Corporate Signatures

Always sign on behalf of the corporation and never yourself, particularly invoices, delivery receipts, contracts or other items of indebtedness, always put the name of the corporation; "by (name of individual)," - and then, following the individual's name, the title. In other words, sign everything "XYZ Corporation, by John Doe, as President" (or Secretary, or Treasurer, or whatever your capacity is). This is giving public notice that you are signing as and for the corporation and not as an individual.

Issue Stock

Issuing stock does not need to be done immediately, but it should be done. Issuing stock is one of those things that corporations do—proprietors and partnerships don't. Again, for your corporation to be treated as a corporation, it needs to act like one-- issue stock sometime during the first year of incorporation. You can issue the stock in exchange for cash, assets or services. Interestingly, Nevada doesn't require its corporations to issue stock, but in California and most other states if you don't issue stock the state considers the corporation to not be capitalized.

Arm's Length

Part of keeping at arm's length from the corporation means that you must take precautions to preserve a legitimate distance from the corporation in order not to have your involvement characterized as an "alter ego" involvement. In order to validate separating yourself from the corporation, you need to make sure that you carry business out legitimately.

Although it is necessary to separate yourself from the corporation, the fact is that any endeavor requires money. Unless you have a slew of investors anxious to hand over their money, chances are that the start-up capital will have to come from your pocket. But your generosity alone is not enough to justify giving the corporation a large sum of money to get started. In this day and age, compensation is the keyword - 'what's in it for me'? This should be the question on your mind because it will be the question on other peoples' minds should your motivation for giving the money ever be questioned.

One way to give the corporation money is through a capital contribution in exchange for stock. Although this would not be ideal for those wanting anonymity, this is a simple and effective way to fund the corporation. The value of the stock increases with the additional capital formation. Start-up capital is non-taxable income, so invest your money wisely.

Another way to move money around is to give a loan to the corporation. In exchange for the funding you give to the corporation, the corporation provides you with a promissory note with specific pay back terms including interest acquired over time. The pay back period may not be immediate; it could be given years from the time of the loan, or it can be on an "on call" basis (this means when you demand payment. A good time would be if the corporation is being sued) but again, being sure that the compensation is reasonable.

Regardless of how the transaction takes place, documentation and compensation of that exchange is key. There must always be a legitimate business reason to support transactions between the corporation and you. But strategies can be very creative as well. For example, if you are interested in purchasing a piece of property, buying a new car, or taking a vacation, you still can, but you must act according to legitimate business reasons.

Keep in mind that the items purchased will not be "yours" per se, but rather you are able to access these items as an employee, agent or affiliate of the corporation. So, let's say that the corporation purchases a corporate car and you, as the vice president carry out important duties on behalf of the business, and consequently, need a car to drive. Although the car is formally registered under the corporate name and owned by that entity, you are allowed to drive the vehicle as a condition of your position within the business. You have just established a legitimate business reason to drive the corporate car. The same basic concept can be applied to taking a vacation (by having a meeting during your trip) or buying a piece of property (for the corporation's future investment). The more creative you are the better, but you need accurate and complete documentation to support these decisions.

Part of providing complete documentation is to make sure those minutes and/or resolutions, checks and other important forms are accurately filled out. It is absolutely necessary to sign the documents with the proper title when you authorize corporate decisions. Let's say you want to buy a piece of property on the corporation's behalf. You authorize the purchase of property, make a resolution, write a check for the given amount and sign it with your name. Transaction complete, right? **Wrong**. By forgetting to sign with **both** your name and your **title**, you have just made a serious mistake. By forgetting to identify your authority to sign such a form, you have subjected the corporation to severe scrutiny. In fact, for such a simple and seemingly insignificant mistake, validating the speculation of its alter-ego status in relation to you may very well pierce the corporation.

Procedures are very important. But just because you cannot buy your groceries with the corporate debit card does not mean that the corporation will not end up paying for your food, should you be able to justify its purchase for a legitimate business reason.

Issuing Stock

All corporations are owned by shareholders. Shareholders make a contribution to the corporation in the form of cash, notes, tangible or intangible property, stock and anything else of value including services (working for the corporation), in exchange for share of ownership (also called "stock shares"), in proportion to the accepted value of the property they contributed. Multiple owners usually agree on the value of any non-cash contributions, but single owners merely put in what they need to operate and are issued shares in return.

As the value of a corporation increases, so too does the value of each share of the corporation's stock. Any additional assets placed into a corporation by its owners will increase the value of the shares in the corporation. The value of a corporation's shares is calculated by determining the difference between a corporation's assets and it liabilities, plus the value of the "good will" of the corporation, divided by the number of issued shares of the corporation.

Every corporation is authorized to issue a certain number of shares of stock. This authorized number of shares is set in the Articles of Incorporation. Of those authorized shares, the corporation's shareholders decide how many shares they will issue. *A corporation's ownership is only based on those shares of the corporation's stock that have been issued*.

Because Nevada keeps the ownership of a corporation a private matter, finding out who the owner is can become quite difficult. If an individual who is filing suit against a corporation is trying to track down a corporation's owner, they will start with the resident agent's office. The resident agent will acknowledge that they represent that corporation. In order to get the documentation that the resident agent has on file (the articles, bylaws and stock ledger statement), there must be a court order from a court of competent jurisdiction **IN NEVADA** to retrieve those documents from the resident agent. This starts them on the trail to the corporate record book, because the document called the "stock ledger statement" tells where the stock ledger, (located in the record book) is kept. The stock ledger should reflect whom the shares of the corporation have been issued to. If your shares have never been issued, it doesn't say anything; but if they catch up with the corporate record book, they have basically caught up with the owner of the corporation, especially if the shares have never been filled out. Even if they weren't filled out but are in your possession, a judge will say that you are the owner of the corporation. If somebody got on the trail of the corporation and went to the resident agent, the resident agent would notify you that somebody was on the trail of the corporation. In the end, anyone seeking information about the corporation will be hard pressed to get it in Nevada.

Types of Stock

No Par Value Stock

No-par stock is the type of stock you receive with most (Nevada) corporations. It has no specific value per share. The Board of Directors has the authority to determine a set value for its no-par value shares. This is done by a corporate resolution.

Common Stock

Common stocks are stock shares that usually possess voting rights and are entitled to dividends as declared by the Board of Directors and to a proportionate share in the distribution of assets at the time of the corporation's liquidation. Because of these ownership characteristics, common stock generally appreciates or depreciates in price according to a corporation's profitability and/or assets.

Voting Stock

This class of stock allows the holder of shares a voting right for each share. Control of the corporation resides in these shares. Common stock is generally issued as voting stock.

Non-Voting Stock

These shares are entitled to a portion of the profits, but they represent no control over operations.

Preferred Stock

Preferred stock is a class of stock with a preference over other forms of stock, normally as to dividends, but sometimes as to voting or liquidation rights.

Cumulative Preferred Stock   This is a class of preferred stock that carries with it a guaranteed return. For instance, the stock may pay out a 10 percent annual dividend, but if the company does not have a good year and there are no profits with which to pay this dividend, the 10 percent accumulates into the next year when, hopefully, there will again be profits.

Convertible Preferred Stock   These are preferred shares that allow the owners to still receive a dividend and allow the owner to convert those shares into common shares and participate in the profits of the company.

Bearer Stock *(Wyoming)*   This is a stock certificate that indicates that the owner of the shares has title to the shares. Bearer shares differ from normal shares in that no records are kept of who owns the shares. Whoever physically holds the bearer share certificates is assumed to be the owner of the shares. This is useful for people who wish to retain anonymity, but ownership is extremely difficult to recover in event of loss or theft.

Ownership vs. Management

Corporate ownership and management consists of three groups of individuals, namely stockholders, directors and officers.

Stockholders

Stockholders (aka shareholders) are the owners of the corporation and holders of the stock certificates. Their primary function related to the corporation is that they elect the Directors. Each share of voting stock is entitled to one vote (That is where control of the corporation comes into play).

Directors are designated to carry out the Stockholders' wishes and run the corporation in the best interests of the Stockholders, with the result of making a profit for distribution to the Stockholders. Stockholders may also elect themselves as Directors, which is usually what happens in small, privately held corporations.

Stockholder Rights

Generally, Stockholders elect and remove Directors, amend the articles and/or corporate bylaws, and approve extraordinary corporate actions. Usually Stockholders have an annual meeting to take care of such business, but a Nevada corporation can accomplish all this business through resolutions.

A Stockholder can either vote his or her shares personally, or someone else authorized to vote the shares through a proxy can vote the shares. In Nevada, a proxy must be in writing, and is generally valid for only 6 months, unless it is either "coupled with an interest" or the Stockholder specifies the length of time the proxy is to remain in force. In either case, the proxy can only be valid for a maximum of 7 years.

Shareholders (aka Stockholders) own the corporation, and this gives them the right to approve or reject extraordinary corporate actions of the board of directors. These actions might include a merger or liquidation. Individually, the shareholders are practically powerless, because they are only entitled to exercise these rights as a group. This means they have to get together in a meeting and vote "yes" or "no" on a particular proposal. Technically this is the extent of the shareholder's role in the corporation.

However, they can hold meetings and vote to approve board proposals. Technically, the shareholders can't, in themselves, carry out a resolution unless they also happen to be the corporation's directors, or officers. But they are then acting as directors or officers and not as Shareholders. If the shareholders can only hold meetings and pass resolutions, it follows that records of meetings and resolutions will help prove that the corporation is being run as a legitimate separate something.

Stockholder Meetings

Most corporate bylaws provide for an annual meeting of shareholders. Generally, the main business at shareholders meetings is to elect a board of directors to serve for the ensuing year. It is also good practice for the shareholders to adopt a resolution ratifying all acts taken by the board of directors during the past year. In addition, specific actions that require shareholder approval, such as an amendment to the articles of incorporation or a merger proposal, also may be taken at the annual meeting.

The procedure to be followed when calling a shareholders meeting is rather standardized throughout the United States. First, the board of directors should adopt a resolution in which it states where and when the meeting is to be held. Next, the board should set a record date, which is the date upon which a person must be a shareholder if he or she is to have the right to vote (Persons acquiring shares after the record date may not vote at the meeting unless they obtain a proxy from the person who sold the shares to them). The board must then have a notice sent to shareholders. This notice must contain the time; date and place of the meeting, and it should list the known agenda for the meeting (if a special meeting is to be held, the notice must state the purpose or purposes for which the meeting is being called).

Occasionally, either the corporation's articles of incorporation or bylaws will specify a time period within those parameters. In such cases, the notice provision in the Corporation document must be followed. A number of states provide that if a corporate action requires a shareholder vote, (e.g., an amendment of the articles of incorporation), the action may be taken without holding a shareholders' meeting if (1) The Corporation obtains a written consent to the action from the shareholders, and (2) the written consent sets out a statement of the action to which the shareholders have consented. Corporations can also use consents if there has been a breakdown or failure in the processes leading up to or taking place during a shareholder meeting, or if through an oversight a meeting was not called and shareholder approval is needed. Where the states differ is in the number of shareholders who must sign consent in order for it to be effective. Delaware, for example, requires the signatures of only a majority of the shareholders entitled to vote on the action, i.e. enough so that if a meeting had been held, the action would have been approved. Other states require the consent to be signed by all shareholders entitled to vote on the matter.

Book of Minutes

As individuals, shareholders are powerless. They can act officially only as a group. This means that they have to get together in a formal meeting before they can legally bind the corporation. There are some exceptions where the shareholders can consent in writing to a particular action without having to hold a meeting.

These instances are rare, and they are usually listed in the articles of incorporation. The following rules and procedures have to be followed for a gathering of shareholders to qualify as an official shareholders meeting:

1. Every shareholder has to be given proper written notice of the date, time and place of the meeting, who is calling the meeting and an agenda of matters that will be considered at the meeting. Virtually every state requires a shareholder to have at least ten days written notice of a meeting. Some states require that shareholders be given no more than 60 days' notice. Notice requirements can be effectively sidestepped in smaller corporations if each shareholder is willing to sign a waiver of notice at the shareholders meeting. The waiver is then attached to the minutes of the meeting.

    Unscheduled or special meetings of shareholders also require written notice although a signed waiver of notice can also be used at these meetings. For an unscheduled meeting to be legally convened, it is essential that the records show that proper notice was given, or that the shareholders signed a waiver of notice requirement. Further, the notice if a special meeting must contain a statement of the meeting's purpose.
    Your articles of incorporation or bylaws will specify where and when a shareholders' meeting can legally be held, and the book of minutes should show the date, time and place of each meeting. In this way, you can prove that the meeting complies with the legal requirements.

2. No business can be transacted at a shareholders' meeting unless a "quorum" is present. Therefore, it is essential that the book of minutes show that a quorum of shareholders attended the meeting. The articles of incorporation or the Bylaws will usually state the size of the quorum, in terms of either the number of shareholders or the number of shares that must be represented at the meeting. For example, a bylaw that says "two-thirds of all shareholders shall constitute a quorum" applies to the number of shareholders and not to the number of shares they own. On the other hand, a bylaw that "a majority of the outstanding stock shall constitute a quorum" means that a certain number of shares of stock must be represented, regardless of whether the stock is owned by one person or by thousands of people.

3. Every shareholders meeting must be presided over by a chairperson. It must also have a secretary to record what happened at the meeting. The bylaws will ordinarily designate these officials, such as by specifying that the president serve as chairperson and the secretary act as secretary. The minutes of each meeting should state who presided at the meeting and who acted as secretary.

4. Parliamentary procedure governs the conduct of meetings. This means that each matter to be acted upon has to be properly introduced by a motion from a member of the group and seconded by another member of the group. Then, every voting member of the group has to be given a chance to vote on the proposal. A sufficient number of votes, usually a majority of the quorum, must be cast in favor of the proposal for it to become binding on the corporation. It is not generally necessary to identify the person making or seconding a motion, nor is it essential to record the exact tally of votes, as long as the outcome is clear to everyone. Language such as "Whereupon, on motion duly made, seconded and carried, it was resolved that" will usually be enough for the minutes to indicate how the manner was handled at the meeting.

5. Each action taken at the meeting should be described in sufficient detail to eliminate ambiguity and disputes over exactly what was agreed upon at the meeting. This is perhaps the most important part of your record keeping chores.

6. Every meeting that has a beginning should also have an end. The end of each meeting should be recorded in the minutes and followed by the signature of the chairperson and secretary of the meeting.

With this record keeping system, therefore, you have all the pertinent documents you will ordinarily need to record the proper and lawful activities of your corporation's shareholders.

Annual Stockholder Meetings

Nevada laws as well as the laws of most states, require that all corporations have annual stockholders' meetings. Aside from annual fees, this is the only other requirement imposed by the state to keep the corporation in good standing. The annual stockholder's meeting usually involves a review of the past year's financial situation, a report by the chairman of the board about the plans for the coming year and a vote naming the people who will be on the next year's Board of Directors.

Board of Directors

The Directors are designated to work for the best interests of the Stockholder and perform accordingly. The Directors are responsible for the general overall management of the corporation. They really have the power to "wheel and deal" with the corporation. They set policy to be carried out by the Officers and make the major decisions of the corporation. They hire the Officers and the Officers take orders from them, usually as directed through the president of the corporation.

The Directors' decisions are decided by voting. However, the Directors do not have one vote per share of stock (they are not necessarily Stockholders); they have one vote each. If there are three Directors, the vote of any two will make a majority or quorum.

Board of Director Meetings

The same considerations that apply to keeping minutes of shareholders' meetings also apply to board meetings. The minutes record the time, place, attendance; agenda and actions taken by the board; together with all the reports, contracts and other documents relevant to the actions taken at the meeting.

At the very first meeting of the board of directors, much of the procedure that the corporation, will follow is established. The bylaws, the corporate seal, stock certificates and record books are adopted, and the company's business is launched. Unlike shareholders' meetings, the procedure for calling a board meeting is not quite so formal as a rule; the articles of incorporation or bylaws of most corporations contain a provision that states when board meetings are to be held. Those provisions constitute notice to each director. If neither the articles of incorporation nor the bylaw contain such a provision, every director must be given reasonable notice of a board meeting. Failure to supply each with reasonable notice will invalidate the meeting.

Annual Board of Director Meetings

The laws of most states require that all corporations have annual board of directors' meetings. Aside from annual fees, this is the only other requirement imposed by the state to keep the corporation in good standing.

The annual Board of Directors meeting generally involves a review of the past year, special reports by directors, nominations of next year's officers and a plan for the next year's growth declaring a dividend (if any), and setting the salary of each officer. If the board takes any additional action, a record of it should be added to the minutes of the meeting, in basically the same format used for the minutes of shareholders' meetings.

Record Keeping

Without the proper corporate record keeping, resolutions and minutes of meetings, as required by law your corporation:

- Could be treated as no corporation at all and the assets, liabilities and tax structure could be recast to you personally (*as a sole proprietorship*).

- You probably will have no protection from personal liability unless you have a viable corporation, which has complied with all state and federal laws.

- The IRS may treat your corporation as no corporation at all recasting the corporation tax returns to your own returns (*as a sole proprietorship*) and denying some of the benefits your corporation is giving to you and your employees.

Record of Director Meetings

Most of the rules and procedures that apply to shareholders' meetings apply equally to meetings of the board of directors. The single most important difference is who is qualified to vote on a particular matter.

With shareholders, voting is a cut-and-dried affair. If they own common stock, they have the right to vote on any matter that comes before the shareholders. Not so with directors. Directors who have an interest in a matter to be voted upon by the board of directors should not vote on the matter. If an interested director does vote, the matter can be voided by the corporation, or by the shareholders unless the interested director can demonstrate (in court if need be) that the transaction was entirely fair to the corporation.

Virtually every state statute provides that a director with a personal interest in the matter may be counted in determining whether a quorum exists; but two cautions should be observed:

1. The interested director should disclose all material information concerning his or her interest in the matter; and

2. The interested director's vote should not be included in determining whether a majority of the board approves of the transaction in question.

Of course, the board still has the responsibility to act in the corporation's best interests. The board cannot put the interests of an individual, even a sole shareholder, above the interests of the corporation. It is the tension between these interests that characterizes the central dilemma of the close corporation.

In practical terms, this means that the corporation's records should show that the actions of the board treat the corporation fairly and that the board has good reasons for the actions it takes. Especially in matters concerning dividends, compensation, contracts and loans to officers and shareholders, it is critically important for the minutes to contain all the arguments, reports, statistics and other documents that can help establish a "reasonable basis" for the board's actions.

With respect to loans, it should be noted that almost every state prohibits a corporation from lending money to a director if that corporation does not also employ the person in some other capacity (e.g., president, vice president or department manager).

At the first board meeting, the board normally adopts a host of resolutions pertaining to how the corporation will conduct its business; what bylaws will be adopted, where the corporation's principal offices will be located, the form of the corporate seal and stock certificates and so on. If any of these resolutions were not adopted by formal resolution at your corporation's first meeting of the board, you should consider doing so at the next board meeting.

Normally, the regular board meeting is concerned only with electing officers for the ensuing year, setting their salaries and other compensation and declaring dividends the actions by the board will require the use of special resolutions. The same considerations that apply to selecting shareholder resolutions apply to the selection and use of board resolutions.

One of the main reasons for keeping records of formal resolutions is that you will occasionally get requests from outside entities such as banks, insurance companies or state agencies for official copies of board or shareholder resolutions. Some will also require an affidavit to be completed by the secretary to certify that the resolution is a true copy of the resolution actually adopted. For this reason, at the end of each document is the text of a standard secretary's certificate. The document has space to imprint the corporate seal, as well as a notary's seal and signature.

Officers

The Officers carry out the instructions of the Board of Directors in the matter of day-to-day basis and make decisions, so long as those decisions are contained within the framework of policy and instructions as handed down by the Board of Directors. The president is in charge of the officers and is the one primarily responsible for reporting to the Board of Directors and insuring that their wishes are carried out.

The responsibilities of both the Directors and Officers are usually spelled out in the Bylaws of the corporation as set down by the Stockholders and/or Directors. The Officers of the corporation are also protected by the corporation from personal liability for acts within the course and scope of their duties. One note of caution, however, officers are responsible for seeing that payroll taxes withheld by the corporation are paid to the IRS. In the event they fail to perform that responsibility, they can be held personally liable and responsible for the payment of those taxes.

Under the laws in most states each corporation shall have a president, a secretary, a treasurer, and a resident agent (The resident agent is the person or company that resides in the state of incorporation who is able to accept "process of service" or other legal service on behalf of the corporation). Here is where many people contemplating a one-person corporation become confused.

The fact is that in a one-person corporation, one person can be each of those offices and be the Director and Stockholder as well. That same person can be president, secretary, and treasurer (however, this is not true in all states). Under Nevada Statutes (NRS 78.130(4)), it specifically states, "any natural person may hold two or more offices."

Employees

The employees are hired by the Officers and carry out their instructions and perform duties consistent with those instructions on a day-to-day basis.

Borrowing Capital

When loaning to your corporation there are some basic rules that need to be understood before you initiate the loan. First of all, the loan must be documented (i.e. a contract and resolution), carry a reasonable interest rate and **must** be repaid on a regular schedule of payments. If this is not done, then the government can re-characterize the loan as a "gift" from you to your corporation. This is something you don't want, as then you can't be reimbursed for the funds you loaned to the corporation.

Secondly, one very good reason for "loaning" money to your corporation is that the documentation you draft concerning the loaned funds becomes a "lien" on the assets of the corporation. Should your corporation be sued, you are in first place to receive the funds or assets held by the corporation. The judgment creditor can only get what is left over after you get paid.

In practical terms, drafting the loan forms means that the corporation's records should show that the actions of the board treat the corporation fairly and that the board has good reasons for the actions it takes.

Loaning Funds to an Officer or Director

When receiving a loan from your corporation there are some basic rules that need to be understood before you take initiate the loan. First of all, the loan must be documented (i.e.' a contract and resolution), carry a reasonable interest rate and **must** be repaid on a regular schedule of payments. If this is not done, then the government can re-characterize the loan as disguised salary that would be taxable as income to you. This is something you don't want especially if you have already filed a tax return showing the funds as a loan.

Secondly, almost every state prohibits a corporation from lending money to a director if that corporation does not also employ the person in some other capacity (e.g., president, vice president or department manager). So if your sole function in your corporation is as a director, be sure that you at least become a vice president. In Nevada, a vice president is not shown on the public records at the Secretary of State. Therefore, even if nominees manage your corporation, you can still be made a Vice President by a simple "appointment" that is placed in the corporate minutes and receive a loan.

Lastly, your corporation can't give you all the funds in the bank either. You must be able to show that the corporation had adequate funds remaining in the bank to undertake it expenses **after** it loans you the money you requested.

In practical terms, this means that the corporation's records should show that the actions of the board treat the corporation fairly and that the board has good reasons for the actions it takes. Especially in matters concerning dividends, compensation, contracts and loans to officers, directors and/or shareholders. It is critically important for the minutes to contain all the arguments, reports, statistics and other documents that can help establish a "reasonable basis" for the board's actions.

Boats, Planes, Vehicles and Other Titled Assets

Property such as boats, planes, vehicles and other titled assets subject to a loan or mortgage in your own personal name can be transferred to an entity in order for you to take the maximum allowable deductions such as writing-off the loan payments, repairs, insurance etc. A corporation can either enter into a loan agreement from a lender, purchase a boat, plane or vehicle from you or rent / lease a vehicle from a leasing company, rental company or from you if you own the vehicle. *Where there is no loan, the information relating to loans and lenders is not applicable and therefore, should be disregarded.*

Purchasing

When purchasing a vehicle from you, any money paid directly to you by the corporation will be taxable to you as income (unless strictly a "re-payment" for money expended within the previous 30-60 days prior to the reimbursement). However, you can have the corporation 'reimburse' you for the money you paid for the vehicle or boat. This reimbursement should not be taxable to you as income. To properly facilitate this, when the corporation reimburses you be sure that in the memo portion of the corporate check you write 'reimbursement only'. Tell your tax person to list the expenditure on the company tax return (this deduction is available to any entity filing an 1120) as you should not claim the reimbursement as income on your personal tax return. When the corporation owns the vehicle all maintenance, insurance and fuel/oil expenses are tax deductible. Please note, you MUST reimburse the corporation for any personal use of the vehicle, boat or plane.

Renting or Leasing

When renting or leasing a vehicle from a rental or leasing company pay with company funds or reimburse your expenditure as soon as corporate funds permit. This expenditure is tax deductible for the corporation. When the corporation rents or leases a vehicle from you that you own outright, any payments paid directly to you by the corporation will be taxable to you as income. However, this expenditure will be deductible for the corporation. Having stated this, there is a way to overcome this predicament by expensing all the maintenance, insurance and other costs to the corporation as reimbursable items.

Drafting Lease or Rental Agreements

If you are making payments toward the lease or purchase of a personal vehicle, you should draft a rental or lease agreement by and between the corporation and you. In the agreement you should state that the loan payment you have to pay is to be paid *directly* to the lender and that all maintenance, insurance and other expenses are to be fully paid or reimbursed to you (should you 'front' the money for the corporation) so that you will not be receiving taxable income from the rental or lease payments. This is applicable when you purchase or lease a vehicle in your personal name for and on behalf of your corporation when the corporation doesn't have the necessary credit to purchase or lease the vehicle on its own. If you are the 'outright' owner of the vehicle (debt-free), you should still draft a rental or lease agreement by and between the corporation and you in the same manner

Seven Important Things to Know About Titling

1. The legal owner will always be the lender (person or entity that provided the money to buy the vehicle) if you or one of your corporations financed (purchased) the vehicle, then you or the corporation should be shown as the legal owner. The "registered owner" would be you or your "home state" corporation that would be using the vehicle.

   Remember that to be able to legally drive and insure the vehicle in your home state the vehicle will have to be registered there. Where the legal owner resides can make a difference to your home state or insurance company.

2. When you have a different legal owner (and a lien on the vehicle), your "home state" corporation simply pays a monthly payment to you or your corporation (the legal owner). In this way, you are moving money from your home state corporation (in a high tax state) to your Nevada (no tax state). This process is called "up streaming" money to a no tax jurisdiction. Oh yes, the payment your "home state" corporation made is 100% tax deductible for the corporation.

3. It is advisable to transfer the title to titled vehicles upon the next scheduled renewal for the vehicle. In other words; when you again must pay for the tags in the case of a vehicle. In this way, you will not have to pay the fees twice in the same year.

4. When transferring the registered ownership (or legal ownership if you own the vehicle out right) at the DMV (or other transferring agency) be sure to let them know that the transfer is simply a change in the way you are holding the title as the "beneficial interest" in the vehicle still will remain the same. By doing this, you might not be charged the sales tax that would otherwise be due and payable at the time of the transfer.

5. The legal owner (lender - if any) would remain the same. Where there is no lender, you would be shown as the lien holder if not fully paid for by the corporation at the time of transfer or if you are leasing or renting the vehicle to your corporation.

6. Be sure to contact your insurance carrier to have the insurance changed to the corporation because, the premiums will be deductible for the corporation. Some carriers don't insure corporate owned boats, planes and vehicles so you may have to shop around, but you should find plenty of carriers from which to chose who do.

However you can be an 'also insured' or you as the driver can be insured with the corporation as the 'also insured'.

7. Remember that when you transfer assets to your corporation, the corporation must compensate you for the equity you already have in the asset. The money the corporation pays to you for that equity in most cases would be taxable to you.

Three Ways for the Corporation to Compensate You for Your Equity

Pay in Cash

The corporation can simply pay you the amount in cash (if it has the money). This would be taxable to you unless the payment(s) are only in reimbursement of funds that you expended in purchasing the vehicle;

Exchange Stock

The corporation can exchange its stock in exchange for the equity in the vehicle. This would be taxable to you; or

Promissory Note

The corporation can give you a promissory note (secured by the equity in the vehicle naturally) in the amount of the equity. This note would be due and payable (with a fair interest rate) upon the sale of the vehicle. The down-side here is that when paid to you, you will have received taxable income. However, this would not be taxable to you should the payment(s) only be a reimbursement of funds that you expended in purchasing the vehicle.

Now anything affecting the vehicle will be for your corporation to handle, as the vehicle is now corporate property. The corporation, will now make the loan payments to the lender, and take the "cash-basis" deductions on its tax return for paying the loan and for all of the expenses associated with the vehicle. The **best** method is to buy in your name on behalf of the corporation and be 'reimbursed' for any funds you paid up front, and have the corporation directly make the payment to the lender.

Asset Protection Services of America

**Universal Documents
Corp · LLC · LP**

ASSIGNMENT

TO WHOM IT MAY CONCERN;

By my signature appearing hereupon, and with full legal right and authority, I the undersigned do hereby assign all my (or rights owned by a company they are a signatory on) rights, interest, obligations and all future income to be derived from *(description of assignments)*:

_____

_____

_____,

is hereby assigned to: _____,

whose mailing address is _____

_____.

Further, this Assignment has been undertaken for and in consideration of;

    A cash payment of $ _____

    A cash payment of $ _____ and promissory note in the amount of

    $ _____ (copy of the note attached).

    A promissory note in the amount of $ _____ (copy of note attached).

    For _____ shares of stock/membership in assignee's company.

    Other _____

This Assignment shall be effective as of the _____ Day of _____ 20___.

IN WITNESS WHEREOF, on this the _____. Day of _____ 20___, I the undersigned hereto set my hand in the execution of this Assignment.

        Authorized Signatory: _____

        Printed Name: _____

(A SIGNED FAXED COPY OF THIS DOCUMENT SHALL BE ACCEPTABLE AS AN ORIGINAL DOCUMENT)

EQUIPMENT LEASE AGREEMENT

Name of Lessee: _____

Address of Lessee: _____

_____

Name of Lessor: _____

Address of Lessor: _____

_____

This is an Agreement to lease the equipment described below. This is not a purchase Agreement as Lessor retains full ownership of the equipment described herein. "Lessor" refers to Lessor named above and/or anyone to whom this lease may be assigned. "Lease" refers to this Lease Agreement. "You" refers to Lessee and any Co-Lessee (if applicable). By signing this Lease Agreement, you agree to all terms and conditions contained herein.

DESCRIPTION OF EQUIPMENT

_____

_____

_____

_____ (*hereinafter referred to as the "Equipment"*).

PRIMARY USAGE WILL BE

_____

_____

_____

1. MONTHLY PAYMENT, PAYMENT DUE DATE AND NUMBER OF LEASE PAYMENTS: The monthly payment amount of $_____ is due and payable on the _____ day of each month, commencing with the month of _____, 20___ , and shall terminate with the _____ monthly Lease payment.

1. (a). LEASE PAYMENT: The Parties hereby agree that all lease payments shall be paid directly to _____

at their mailing address of _____
_____.

2. RISK OF LOSS: You will have the risk of loss of the Equipment once you take possession of it, except should the Equipment be stolen (***and not recovered***) or destroyed and there is an insurance settlement paid to Lessor in the full amount then owing.

3. MAINTENANCE, REPAIRS, AND OPERATING EXPENSES: You agree to maintain and repair the Equipment and to keep it in good working order and condition. You agree to pay for all maintenance, repair, and all operating expenses of said Equipment. If you do not maintain or repair the Equipment as this Lease requires, Lessor may do so and add the cost to your obligation under this Lease.

4. FINES, LIENS, AND ENCUMBRANCES: You agree to keep the Equipment free of all fines, liens, and encumbrances. If you do not promptly pay any fines or remove any liens or encumbrances (if applicable), Lessor may do so. Should Lessor pay any fines or remove any liens or encumbrances, You agree to promptly reimburse Lessor for any amounts Lessor pays on Your behalf.

5. DEFAULT: You will be in default if any of the following occurs:

- You do not make a payment when due.
- You make an assignment for the benefit of creditors.
- You do not keep insurance coverage on the Equipment.
- You do not repair or maintain the Equipment.
- You transfer your interest in this lease.
- You die during the lease term.
- You break any of your other agreements in this Lease and such breach significantly impairs the prospect of payment, performance, or realization of Lessor's interest in the Equipment.
- You do any other act that is considered a default under a lease contract under applicable law.

6. IF YOU ARE IN DEFAULT: If you are in default, Lessor may terminate this Lease, and repossess the Equipment. In addition, you may be subject to suit and liability for the unpaid indebtedness evidenced by this Agreement.

7. AT THE END OF THE LEASE: You agree to return the Equipment in good condition, at the end of the Lease to the address Lessor gives you and you will owe no other fees or payments, unless you desire to buy the Equipment. You have the option to purchase the Equipment only at the end of the Lease. The purchase price shall be established as the fair market value of the Equipment at the end of the term of the Lease.

8. PROHIBITION OF TRANSFER OF LESSEE'S INTEREST: You will not sublease, rent assign, grant a security interest in or otherwise transfer your interest under this Lease in a way that affects your possession or use of the Equipment or any other right in the Equipment, nor will you attempt to transfer any other right or interest under this Lease or in the Equipment. However, Lessor, upon request, may give prior written consent to a transfer.

9. INDEMNITY: You will protect Lessor, and anyone to whom Lessor assigns this Lease, from all losses, damages, injuries, claims, demands, and expenses arising out of the condition, maintenance, use, or operation of the Equipment. In addition, you agree to indemnify and hold Lessor and its assigns harmless from any and all losses, damages, injuries, claims, demands, and expenses.

10. DELIVERY RECEIPT: By signing this Lease, you agree that **(i)** You received and examined the Equipment described in this Lease, **(ii)** the Equipment is as described in this Lease, and **(iii)** the Equipment is in good working order and condition.

11. ENTIRE AGREEMENT: This Lease contains the entire Agreement between You and Lessor. There are no other agreements between You and Lessor, except those written in this Lease. No course of performance will be used to determine the meaning of this Lease or to show a change to this Lease and no changes to this Lease will be valid unless committed to writing and signed by You and Lessor.

12. ADDITIONAL CONDITIONS:

_____

_____

_____

13. WARRANT: The undersigned warrants that they fully understand their legal rights and obligations in connection herewith and that having understood the obligations detailed herein, has without any reservation, executed this instrument on this the _____. Day of _____ 20___.

Lessee Signature: _____

Printed Name: _____

Lessor Signature: _____

Printed Name: _____

GENERAL ASSIGNMENT

TO WHOM IT MAY CONCERN:

By my signature appearing hereupon, and with full legal right and authority, I the undersigned do hereby assign all my (*or rights owned by a company they are a signatory on*) rights, interest, obligations and all future income to be derived from _____ (put in a description of what is being assigned)_____

_____

_____, is hereby assigned to

_____,

whose address is _____

_____.

Further, this Assignment has been undertaken for and in consideration of;

_____ A cash payment of $ _____

_____ A cash payment of $ _____ and a promissory note in the amount of _____ ($_____) (copy of the note attached).

_____ A promissory note in the amount of $ _____ (copy of note attached).

_____ For _____ shares of stock (membership) in assignee's Company.

_____ Other _____

This Assignment shall be effective as of the _____ Day of _____ 20___.

IN WITNESS WHEREOF, on this the _____. Day of _____ 20___, I the undersigned hereto set my hand in the execution of this Assignment.

Printed Name: _____

Authorized Signatory: _____

(A SIGNED FAXED COPY OF THIS DOCUMENT SHALL BE ACCEPTABLE AS AN ORIGINAL DOCUMENT)

LEASE AGREEMENT

THIS LEASE AGREEMENT is entered into this _____ day of _____, 20___, by and between _____

_____ (*hereinafter referred to as "Landlord"*), whose address is _____

_____, and _____,

whose address is _____,

_____(*Hereinafter referred to as "Tenant"*).

1.   Landlord leases to Tenant and Tenant leases from Landlord, upon the terms and conditions contained herein, the dwelling located at _____

_____,

for the period commencing on the first day of _____, 20___, and thereafter until the first day of _____, 20___, at which time this Lease Agreement shall terminate, be renewed or be continued on a month to month basis by agreement of the parties hereto.

2.   Tenant shall pay as rent the sum of _____ ($_____)
Dollars per month, due and payable monthly, in advance, no later than 5:00 p.m. on the fifth day of every month. Regardless of the cause Tenant further agrees to pay a late charge of $5.00 to the Landlord for each day thereafter, that the Landlord does not receive rent. In additional a service charge of $20.00 will be paid by Tenant to Landlord, for any and all bank dishonored checks.

3.   Tenant agrees to accept the property in its current condition and to return it in *"moving-in clean"* condition, or to pay a special cleaning charge of _____
($_____) upon vacating the premises.

4.   Tenant agrees to pay a Security Deposit of _____ ($_____)
to secure Tenant's pledge of full compliance with the terms of this Agreement.

5.   Tenant warrants that any work or repairs performed by resident will be undertaken only if he/she/it is competent and qualified to perform the work. If such work is undertaken, tenant shall be totally responsible for all activities to assure that work is done in a safe manner and shall meet all applicable codes and statutes. Tenant further warrants that he/she/it shall be accountable for any mishaps and/or accidents resulting from such work, and shall hold Landlord free from harm, litigation, or claims of any other person.

6.   Tenant will be responsible for maintaining the premises and grounds in a satisfactory manner. This includes lawn care, trimming shrubbery and watering lawn as necessary.

7.   All problems shall be reported to the, Landlord. Any and all *"Services"*, if they are required, will be ordered by the Landlord, and **NOT BY TENANT**, unless Tenant will be responsible for payment of those services, and such payment may not be deducted from lease payments due and owing unless authorized in writing by the Landlord. Tenant shall do no painting or remodeling without the express consent of the Landlord.

8.   All matters pertaining to this Lease Agreement shall be governed by, construed and enforced in accordance with the laws of the State of _____. The parties herein waive trial by jury and the personal jurisdiction and venue of a court of subject matter jurisdiction located in _____ County, in the State of _____. In the event that litigation results from or arises out of this Agreement or the performance hereof, the parties agree to reimburse the prevailing party's reasonable attorney's fees, court costs, and all other expenses, whether or not taxable by the court as costs, in addition to any other relief to which the prevailing party may be entitled. In such event, no action shall be entertained by said court or any court of competent jurisdiction if filed more than one year subsequent to the date the cause(s) of action actually accrued, regardless of whether damages were otherwise as of said time, calculable.

9. Landlord acknowledges that the above named property is leased primarily as an **OFFICE LOCATION** for document processing in the above named State. However, in order to protect the property of Landlord and Tenant, a company officer shall maintain a physical presence at the above named location on a full time basis. However, Tenant agrees that Landlord shall retain the right to approve or disapprove of the officer(s) who are to occupy the above named premises.

10. Landlord acknowledges and agrees that Tenant shall not be responsible for the care or for any damage, no matter the cause, to Landlord's personal property (*or any other person(s), if any*), which left at the above named location.

11. Both parties agree that to be valid and binding, this Lease Agreement and any and all addendum's (*if any*), **MUST** be signed by both parties.

PERSONAL GUARANTEE OF PAYMENT

I the undersigned, personally guarantee the payment of the above stated lease payments for the period contemplated by this Lease.

IN WITNESS WHEREOF, on the date first written above, we the undersigned hereto set our hands in the execution of this Agreement.

TENANT   Name: _____   Signature: _____

          ID Number: _____   Type of ID:_____

          Place of issue: _____   State:_____

LANDLORD Name: _____   Signature: _____

MANAGEMENT SERVICE AGREEMENT

THIS MANAGEMENT SERVICE AGREEMENT is a private agreement, entered into on this the
_____. day of _____ 20___ by and between the following Parties:

COMPANY: _____

Street Address: _____

_____

Phone: _____

Fax / e-fax: _____

Mobile: _____

E-Mail: _____

Represented By: _____

SERVICE PROVIDER: _____

Street Address: _____

_____

Phone: _____

Fax / e-fax: _____

Mobile: _____

E-Mail: _____

Represented By: _____

(*Hereinafter referred to as the "Parties" or in their individual designations*).

WITNESSETH

WHEREAS, Company desires to engage the services of Service Provider, to manage Company (a Limited Liability Company), (*hereinafter referred to as the Project*); and,

WHEREAS, Service Provider agrees to undertake the above mentioned Project for Company by whatever means Service Provider chooses; and,

NOW, THEREFORE, in consideration of the promises, covenants and conditions herein contained, the Parties hereby mutually agree as follows:

1. **TERM:** The respective duties and obligations of the contracting Parties shall be for twelve (12) month(s), commencing on the date first written above. After this term, this Agreement shall be automatically renewed for successive twelve (12) monthly periods, unless terminated by either party by providing written notice to the other party, no less than five (5) business days prior to the initial or renewal termination date.

2. **SERVICES AND/OR CONSULTATIONS:** Service Provider shall provide its services and/or consult with the heads of the administrative staff of Company and/or the membership of Company, at reasonable times during the normal business hours of Company. In addition, Service Provider hereby agrees that he/she/it shall be available at such times and places beyond normal business hours when reasonably necessary, to address matters relating to the Project.

3. **LIABILITY:** The Parties hereto agree that with regard to the duties and/or services to be rendered by each party pursuant to the terms of this Agreement, each party shall be solely liable to anyone who may claim any right due to any acts or omissions in the performance of their respective duties and/or services or on the part of their respective agents, contractors or employees. In this same regard, the answerable party shall hold the other party free and harmless from any obligations, costs, claims, judgments, attorneys' fees and/or attachments arising from, or growing out of their respective services as rendered pursuant to the terms of this Agreement.

4. **COMPENSATION:** For undertaking the above-referenced Project, Company agrees to compensate Service Provider as follows: _____

_____

_____.

4.1. **COMPENSATION PAYMENT DATE:** Company agrees to compensate Service Provider (*as stated in Section 4. above*), on a monthly basis commencing on _____20___ or at a pre determined time by the written or verbal agreement of the Parties.

5. **TERMINATION:** Either party may terminate and cancel this Agreement and bring the business relationship contemplated herein to a close (*Other than as stated in Section 1 above*)

at any time for any reason, by giving five (5) business days notice of termination to the other party.

6. INDEPENDENT BUSINESS RELATIONSHIP: The Parties are, and shall be deemed to be independent businesses with the sole right to perform their respective services under this Agreement. Nothing in this Agreement shall be deemed or construed to create a partnership, joint venture, an employer/employee relationship, a principal/agent relationship, or to otherwise create any liability for the other party whatsoever, with respect to the indebtedness, liabilities or other obligations of the other party or any party, except as otherwise specifically set forth herein.

7. TAXES: Unless otherwise specifically provided herein, the Parties hereby agree that the Parties shall each be liable and responsible for any and all taxes attributable to them, their employees, agents and/or their representatives under this Agreement, which may be deemed to be owed by them individually.

8. COMPETITION AND NON COMPETE: Service Provider may engage in any other activities it desires, even if such activities are related to the services performed by Service Provider for Company under this Agreement.

9. GOOD FAITH: Each party shall promote and execute this Agreement with diligence, utmost good faith and loyalty to the other party.

10. ATTORNEY & OTHER LEGAL FEES: Both Parties hereby agree that in the event that either party commences an action at law or in equity against the other to enforce any of the terms, conditions, covenants, promises or provisions of this Agreement by reason of a breach or default hereunder, the party prevailing in any such action shall be entitled to, and receive all reasonable attorney's fees and other such costs from the other party.

11. WARRANT: Each party, and each person signing on behalf of a party, represents and warrants that they have the full legal capacity and authority to enter into and perform the obligations of this Agreement without any further approval.

12. INVALIDITY OF PARTICULAR PROVISION(S): In the event that any portion of this Agreement shall, for any reason, be deemed to be invalid or unenforceable, the remaining portions of this Agreement shall be fully effective, valid and enforceable.

13. VENUE, SUCCESSORS & ASSIGNS: Both Parties hereby agree that the venue for the terms, conditions of this Agreement shall be _____ County in the State of _____, or as the Parties may agree at a later date, and shall inure to the benefit of, and be binding upon heirs, successors and assigns of the Parties hereto.

14. ENTIRE AGREEMENT: This Agreement contains the entire agreement between the Parties hereto. No modifications, amendments or changes in any of the terms, conditions or provisions hereof shall be valid unless signed by both Parties and attached hereto as an amendment.

15. NOTICES: All notices and other communications under this Agreement, must be in writing, and if mailed, must be mailed by registered or certified mail, or delivered by hand to the party to whom such notice is required to be given. If mailed, any such notice shall be considered to have been given three (3) business days after it was mailed, as evidenced by the postmark. If delivered by hand, when receive by the party, or their representative, as evidenced by a written and dated receipt of the receiving party. The mailing address for notice to either party shall be the address shown herein.

16. PROPRIETARY RIGHTS & CONFIDENTIALITY: Both Parties acknowledge that during the term covered by this Agreement, each Party shall have access to and become acquainted with various trade secrets, inventions, innovations, processes, information, records and specifications owned or licensed and/or used by the other Party in connection with the operation of its business including, without limitation, the other Party's business and product processes, methods, customer lists, accounts and procedures.

All files, records, documents, blueprints, specifications, information, letters, notes, media lists, original artwork, creative work, notebooks, and similar items relating to the business (hereinafter referred to as "materials") of either Party, shall remain the exclusive property of the creating and/or providing Party. Upon the expiration or earlier termination of this Agreement, or whenever requested by either party, both Parties shall immediately deliver to the other Party all such files, records, documents, specifications, information, and other items in his/her/its possession or under his or her control belonging to the other Party.

Additionally, Company hereby agrees to immediately terminate its use (in any manner whatsoever) of any and all of the materials Service Provider has provided and/or shared with Company upon the termination of this Agreement, unless Service Provider authorizes the contrary in writing.

17. PROPRIETARY RIGHTS & CONFIDENTIALITY - RIGHT TO INJUNCTION: The Parties hereto acknowledge that the services to be rendered by Service Provider under this Agreement and the rights and privileges granted by Company under the Agreement are of a special, unique, unusual, and extraordinary character which gives them a peculiar value, the loss of which cannot be reasonably or adequately compensated by damages in any action at law, and the breach by either Party of any of the provisions of this Agreement will cause the other Party irreparable injury and damage.

Therefore, the Parties expressly agree that the damaged Party shall be entitled to injunctive and other equitable relief in the event of, or to prevent, a breach of any provision of this Agreement by the other Party. Failure by the damaged Party to resort to such equitable relief shall not be constructed to be a waiver of any other rights or remedies that the damaged Party may have for damages. The various rights and remedies of the damaged Party under this Agreement or otherwise shall be constructed to be cumulative, and no one of them shall be exclusive of any other or of any right or remedy allowed by law.

18. FACSIMILE OF THIS DOCUMENT: Unless specifically referenced herein, a signed facsimile of this document shall be legally binding as though it was an original instrument.

19. ADDITIONAL TERMS AND CONDITIONS: The Parties hereby agree to the following additional terms and conditions:

_____

_____

_____

_____

IN WITNESS WHEREOF, The undersigned confirm that they are the authorized representatives of their respective entities. Further, they warrant that they fully understand their legal rights and obligations in connection herewith and that having understood these legal rights and obligations, have without any reservation, agreed to be bound by this Agreement as of the date first written above.

FOR AND ON BEHALF OF **COMPANY**

Authorized Signatory: _____

Printed Name: _____

FOR AND ON BEHALF OF **SERVICE PROVIDER**

Authorized Signatory: _____

Printed Name: _____

*(**Put on personal or business letterhead**)*

PROMISSORY NOTE

Amount of Note: $_____

Maturity Date For Payment Of Principal: _____ day of _____, 20____

For value received, I/we the undersigned (the issuer of the note) hereby irrevocably and unconditionally without protest or notification, promise to pay against this Promissory Note, to the order of (the beneficiary of this note), the bearer or holder hereof, annually in arrears the sum of _____ ($_____) In lawful currency of the United States upon presentation and surrender of this Promissory Note at the offices of (**location for payment**).

Such payment shall be made without setoff and free and clear of any deductions or charges, fees or withholdings of any kind now or hereafter imposed, levied, collected, withheld or assessed by the United States government or any political subdivision or authority thereof.

This Promissory Note is divisible, transferable and assignable without presentation to us or the payment of any transfer fees of any kind.

This Promissory Note shall be governed by, and shall be construed in adherence with the laws of the State of _____ and the United States of America.

IN WITNESS WHEREOF I/we have set our hand(s) hereupon on this the _____ Day of _____ 20____

Signature of Maker: _____

Printed Name: _____

ID #: _____ Type: _____

Signature of Maker: _____

Printed Name: _____

ID #: _____ Type: _____

REAL ESTATE SERVICE AGREEMENT

THIS REAL ESTATE SERVICE AGREEMENT is entered into by and between:

SERVICE PROVIDER(S)	**CLIENT #1**
Mailing Address:	Client Address
SERVICE PROVIDER(S)	**CLIENT #2**
Mailing Address:	Client Address

and

COMPANY	**COMPANY NAME**
Address:	Company Business Address
Represented By:	Authorized Signatory

(Hereinafter collectively referred to as The PARTIES or by their individual designations).

WITNESSETH

WHEREAS, Company, *(Name of State)* desires to engage the services of Service Provider(s) to purchase or otherwise acquire the following real estate on behalf of Company:

(Complete Property Address)
(Property Parcel Number)

WHEREAS, Company agrees that for the life of the "loan" (mortgage), Company shall pay all mortgage payments, utilities, insurance and any and all other costs and/or expenses associated with said property; and

WHEREAS, Service Provider(s) agree to 'take title' to said property in their personal name(s) as soon as practical after receiving the title, Service Provider(s) agrees to assign (transfer) all future equity and income derived from said property to Company by assigning (transferring) said 'title' to Company; and,

WHEREAS, Service Provider(s) agree to personally remain wholly liable for any and all 'loans' (debts) relating to said property as the sole '*BORROWER OF RECORD*'; and

NOW, THEREFORE, in consideration of the promises, covenants and conditions herein contained the parties on their own behalf or on behalf of an entity to be named later by the Parties, agree to mutually undertake this 'venture' under the following terms and conditions:

1. DEFINITIONS:

(A) Service Provider(s) shall be defined as the sole Beneficial Interest holder(s) (owners) of the Company and the property named herein.

(B) Company shall be defined as the 'entity' (investment vehicle) chosen by the Beneficial Interest holder(s) to hold all rights, title and interest in connection with the future equity and or income derived from the above-mentioned 'property'.

2.	**TERM:** The respective duties and obligations of the contracting parties and shall commence on the date first written above and shall remain in effect for as long as said property stay in the name of the Company.

3.	**REIMBURSEMENT OF OUT OF POCKET EXPENSES:** Company hereby agrees to reimburse Service Provider(s) for any moneys he/she/it had 'advanced' in acquiring the above-mentioned property and for any moneys he/she/it may 'advance' in the payment of any expense or fee relating to said property after its transfer to Company.

4.	**LIABILITY:** The parties hereby agree that with regard to the duties and/or services to be rendered by each party pursuant to the terms of this Agreement, each party shall be solely liable to anyone who may claim any right due to any acts or omissions in the performance of their respective duties and/or services or on the part of their respective agents, contractors or employees. In this same regard, the answerable party shall hold the other party free and harmless from any obligations, costs, claims, judgments, attorneys' fees and/or attachments arising from, or growing out of their respective services as rendered pursuant to the terms of this Agreement.

5.	**TERMINATION:** Either party may only terminate this Agreement (*Other than as stated in Section 1 above*), for the misconduct, negligence or for failure to comply with the conditions, covenants, promises or provisions contained in this Agreement.

6.	**TAXES:** Unless otherwise specifically provided herein, the parties hereby agree that both parties shall be solely liable and responsible for any and all taxes attributable to them or their employees, agents, or representatives under this Agreement.

7.	**GOOD FAITH:** Each party shall promote and execute this Agreement with diligence, utmost good faith and loyalty to the other party.

8.	**ATTORNEY & OTHER LEGAL FEES:** Both parties hereby agree that in the event that either party commences an action at law or in equity against the other to enforce any of the terms, conditions, covenants, promises or provisions of this Agreement by reason of a breach or default thereunder, the party prevailing in any such action or proceedings shall be entitled to, and receive all reasonable attorney's fees and other such costs from the other party.

9.	**WARRANT:** Each party, and each person signing on behalf of a party, represents and warrants that they have the full legal capacity and authority to enter into and perform the obligations of this Agreement without any further approval.

10.   INVALIDITY OF PARTICULAR PROVISION(S): In the event that any portion of this Agreement shall, for any reason, be deemed to be invalid or unenforceable, the remaining portions of this Agreement shall be fully effective, valid and enforceable.

11.   VENUE, SUCCESSORS & ASSIGNS: Both parties hereby agree that the venue for the terms, conditions and provisions of this Agreement shall be in the State of Nevada or as the parties may agree at a later date, and shall inure to the benefit of, and be binding upon heirs, successors and assigns of the parties hereto.

12.   ENTIRE AGREEMENT: This Agreement contains the entire agreement between the parties hereto. No modifications, amendments or changes in any of the terms, conditions or provisions hereof shall be valid unless signed by both parties and attached hereto as an amendment.

13.   NOTICES: All notices and other communications under this Agreement must be in writing, and if mailed, any such notice shall be considered to have been given three (3) business days after it was mailed, as evidenced by the postmark. The mailing address for notice to either party shall be the address shown herein.

14.   FAXED COPIES: The parties agree that a signed "FAXED" copy of this document shall be acceptable as an original document and thereby legally binding on both parties.

IN WITNESS WHEREOF, this Agreement has been executed by each of the individual parties hereto and signed by an officer, duly authorized of the Company party hereto, (*if applicable*), all on the date and year first above written.

REAL ESTATE SERVICE AGREEMENT

SERVICE PROVIDER(S)

_____
Client #1

_____
Client #2

NOTARY ACKNOWLEDGEMENT

STATE OF _____)
) SS.
COUNTY OF _____)

On _____ before me, _____
                                                            (insert name and title of the officer)

personally appeared _____, and

personally appeared _____, who proved to me on the basis of satisfactory evidence to be the person(s) whose name(s) is are subscribed to the within instrument and acknowledged to me that he/she/they executed the same in his/her/their authorized capacity(ies), and that by his/her/their signature(s) on the instrument the person(s), or the entity upon behalf of which the person(s) acted, executed the instrument.

I certify under PENALTY OF PERJURY under the laws of the State of _____ that the foregoing paragraph is true and correct.

WITNESS my hand and official seal.

_____
Notary Public Signature

REAL ESTATE SERVICE AGREEMENT

COMPANY

_____

Represented by

NOTARY ACKNOWLEDGEMENT

STATE OF _____)
) SS.
COUNTY OF _____)

On _____ before me, _____

(insert name and title of the officer)

personally appeared _____, who proved to me on the basis of satisfactory evidence to be the person(s) whose name(s) is are subscribed to the within instrument and acknowledged to me that he/she/they executed the same in his/her/their authorized capacity(ies), and that by his/her/their signature(s) on the instrument the person(s), or the entity upon behalf of which the person(s) acted, executed the instrument.

I certify under PENALTY OF PERJURY under the laws of the State of _____ that the foregoing paragraph is true and correct.

WITNESS my hand and official seal.

_____

Notary Public Signature

SERVICE AGREEMENT

This **SERVICE AGREEMENT** is a private agreement, entered into on this the _____ day of _____ 20____ under the Constitutions and Common Laws of the United States and the State of _____, by and between the following Parties:

COMPANY: _____

Street Address: _____

_____

Phone: _____

Fax / e-fax: _____

Mobile: _____

E-Mail: _____

Represented By: _____

SERVICE PROVIDER: _____

Street Address: _____

_____

Phone: _____

Fax / e-fax: _____

Mobile: _____

E-Mail: _____

Represented By: _____

(*Hereinafter referred to as the "Parties" or in their individual designations*).

WITNESSETH

WHEREAS, Company desires to engage the services of Service Provider(s), to:

_____

_____

_____

_____

_____ (*hereinafter referred to as the 'Project'*); and,

WHEREAS, Service Provider(s), on their own behalf or on behalf of an entity(ies) to be named later by Service Provider(s), agrees to undertake the above mentioned Project for Company; and,

NOW, THEREFORE, in consideration of the promises, covenants and conditions herein contained, the parties hereby mutually agree as follows:

1. TERM: The respective duties and obligations of the contracting parties shall be for _____ (___) month(s), commencing on the date first written above. After this term, this Agreement shall be automatically renewed for successive _____ (___) monthly periods, unless terminated by either party by providing written notice to the other party, no less than fourteen (14) days prior to the initial or renewal termination date.

2. SERVICES AND/OR CONSULTATIONS: Service Provider(s) shall provide its services and/or consult with the Board of Directors, the officers and/or the heads of the administrative staff of Company, at reasonable times and/or during the normal business hours of Company. In addition, Service Provider(s) hereby agrees that he/she/it shall be available at such times and places beyond normal business hours when reasonably necessary, to address matters relating to the Project.

3. LIABILITY: The parties hereby agree that with regard to the duties and/or services to be rendered by each party pursuant to the terms of this Agreement, each party shall be solely liable to anyone who may claim any right due to any acts or omissions in the performance of their respective duties and/or services or on the part of their respective agents, contractors or employees. In this same regard, the answerable party shall hold the other party free and harmless from any obligations, costs, claims, judgments, attorneys' fees and/or attachments arising from, or growing out of their respective services as rendered pursuant to the terms of this Agreement.

4. COMPENSATION: For undertaking the above mentioned Project, Company agrees to compensate Service Provider(s) as follows: _____

_____

_____

_____

4.1. COMPENSATION PAYMENT DATE: Company agrees to compensate Service Provider(s) (*as stated in Section 4. above*), within ten (10) days of their receipt of an invoice or other billing instrument for same or at a pre determined time by the written or verbal agreement of the parties.

5. COMPANY TERMINATION: Company may **ONLY** terminate this Agreement (*Other than as stated in Section 1 above*):

(a). For the misconduct, negligence or for Service Provider(s) failure to comply with the conditions, covenants, promises or provisions contained in this Agreement.

(b). For the failure of Service Provider(s) to provide Its services under this Agreement, provided however, in the event Service Provider(s) defaults in the performance of any agreement made hereunder, Service Provider(s) shall have an agreement to remedy such breach to Company's satisfaction within ten (10) business days notice and demand by Company.

5.1. SERVICE PROVIDER(S) TERMINATION: Service Provider(s) may terminate this Agreement without recourse by Company (*Other than as stated in Section 1 above*):

(a). For the misconduct, negligence or for Companies failure to comply with the conditions, covenants, promises or provisions contained in this Agreement.

(b). For the failure of Company to provide Its services under this Agreement, provided however, in the event Company defaults in the performance of any agreement made hereunder, Company shall have an agreement to remedy such breach to Service Provider(s) satisfaction within ten (10) business days notice and demand by Service Provider(s).

6. INDEPENDENT BUSINESS RELATIONSHIP: The parties are, and shall be deemed to be independent businesses with the sole right to perform their respective services under this Agreement. Nothing in this Agreement shall be deemed or construed to create a partnership, joint venture, an employer/employee relationship, a principal/agent relationship, or to otherwise create any liability for the other party whatsoever, with respect to the indebtedness, liabilities or other obligations of the other party or any party, except as otherwise specifically set forth herein.

7. TAXES: Unless otherwise specifically provided herein, the parties hereby agree that Service Provider(s) shall be solely liable and responsible for any and all taxes attributable to Service Provider(s), its employees, agents, or representatives under this Agreement, which may be deemed to be owed by Service Provider(s).

8. COMPETITION: Service Provider(s) may engage in any other activities it desires, even if such activities are related to the services performed by Service Provider(s) for Company under this Agreement. However, Service Provider(s) shall not contract another business offering the same business activity as Company, during the term covered by this Agreement.

9. GOOD FAITH: Each party shall promote and execute this Agreement with diligence, utmost good faith and loyalty to the other party.

10. TOOLS, EQUIPMENT, SUPPLIES & SPACE: The parties hereby agree that in order to maintain uniformity and meet the legal requirements governing the business of Company, Company shall, without charge to Service Provider(s), make tools, equipment, supplies and space, available to Service Provider(s) to facilitate Service Provider(s) contracted services whenever the fulfillment of same are necessary to be accomplished on the business premises of Company.

11. ATTORNEY & OTHER LEGAL FEES: Both parties hereby agree that in the event that either party commences an action at law or in equity against the other to enforce any of the terms, conditions, covenants, promises or provisions of this Agreement by reason of a breach or default hereunder, the party prevailing in any such action or proceedings shall be entitled to, and receive all reasonable attorney's fees and other such costs from the other party. In the event such prevailing party secures a judgment, all such fees shall be included in said judgment and shall be set by the court and not a jury.

12. WARRANT: Each party, and each person signing on behalf of a party, represents and warrants that they have the full legal capacity and authority to enter into and perform the obligations of this Agreement without any further approval.

13. INVALIDITY OF PARTICULAR PROVISION(S): In the event that any portion of this Agreement shall, for any reason, be deemed to be invalid or unenforceable, the remaining portions of this Agreement shall be fully effective, valid and enforceable.

14. VENUE, SUCCESSORS & ASSIGNS: Both parties hereby agree that the venue for the terms, conditions and provisions of this Agreement shall be the State of _____, or as the parties may agree at a later date, and shall inure to the benefit of, and be binding upon heirs, successors and assigns of the parties hereto.

15. ENTIRE AGREEMENT: This Agreement contains the entire agreement between the parties hereto. No modifications, amendments or changes in any of the terms, conditions or provisions hereof shall be valid unless signed by both parties and attached hereto as an amendment.

16. NOTICES: All notices and other communications under this Agreement, must be in writing, and if mailed, must be mailed by registered or certified mail, or delivered by hand to the party to whom such notice is required to be given. If mailed, any such notice shall be considered to have been given three (3) business days after it was mailed, as evidenced by the postmark. If delivered by hand, when receive by the party, or their representative, as evidenced by a written and dated receipt of the receiving party. The mailing address for notice to either party shall be the address shown herein.

17. ADDITIONAL TERMS AND CONDITIONS: The parties hereby agree to the following additional terms and conditions:

(a). The parties hereby agree that Initially, the person who will fulfill the obligations of the Service Provider(s) under this Agreement shall be: _____.

(b). _____

_____

_____

IN WITNESS WHEREOF, this Agreement has been executed by each of the individual parties hereto and signed by an officer, duly authorized of the company hereto, (*if applicable*), all on the date and year first above written.

SERVICE PROVIDER(S)

Signed: _____

Title: _____

Printed Name: _____

EIN # or SS #: _____

COMPANY

Signed: _____

Printed Name: _____

Title: _____

VEHICLE LEASE AGREEMENT

Name of Lessee : _____

Address of Lessee: _____

_____

Name Of Lessor : _____

Address Of Lessor: _____

_____

This is an Agreement to lease the Vehicle described below. This is not a purchase Agreement as Lessor retains full ownership of the Vehicle described herein. "Lessor" refers to Lessor named above and/or anyone to whom this lease may be assigned. "Lease" refers to this Lease Agreement. "You" refers to Lessee and any Co-Lessee (if applicable). By signing this Lease Agreement, you agree to all terms and conditions contained herein.

DESCRIPTION OF VEHICLE

Year, Make and Model: _____

License Number _____

V.I.N. _____

Purchase From: _____

Purchase price of: $_____

To be paid in: _____ Cash _____ Credit _____ Other: _____

(Hereinafter referred to as the "Vehicle").

PRIMARY USAGE WILL BE

_____

_____

_____

1. MONTHLY PAYMENT, PAYMENT DUE DATE AND NUMBER OF LEASE PAYMENTS: The monthly payment amount of $_____ is due and payable on the _____ day of each month, commencing with the month of _____, 20___ , and shall terminate with the _____ monthly Lease payment.

1. 1. LEASE PAYMENT: The Parties hereby agree that all lease payments shall be paid directly to _____ **(generally the lender of Lessor)** at their mailing address of _____ _____.

2. RISK OF LOSS: You will have the risk of loss of the Vehicle once you take possession of it, except should the Vehicle be stolen (***and not recovered***) or destroyed and there is an insurance settlement paid to Lessor in the full amount then owing.

3. MAINTENANCE, REPAIRS, AND OPERATING EXPENSES: You agree to maintain and repair the Vehicle and to keep it in good working order and condition. You agree to pay for all maintenance, repair, and all operating expenses of said Vehicle. If you do not maintain or repair the Vehicle as this Lease requires, Lessor may do so and add the cost to your obligation under this Lease.

4. FINES, LIENS, AND ENCUMBRANCES: You agree to keep the Vehicle free of all fines, liens, and encumbrances. If you do not promptly pay any fines or remove any liens or encumbrances (if applicable), Lessor may do so. Should Lessor pay any fines or remove any liens or encumbrances, you agree to promptly reimburse Lessor for any amounts Lessor pays on your behalf.

5. DEFAULT: You will be in default if any of the following occurs:

- You do not make a payment when due.
- You make an assignment for the benefit of creditors.
- You do not keep insurance coverage on the Vehicle.
- You do not repair or maintain the Vehicle.
- You transfer your interest in this lease.
- You die during the lease term.
- You break any of your other agreements in this Lease and such breach significantly impairs the prospect of payment, performance, or realization of Lessor's interest in the Vehicle.
- You do any other act that is considered a default under a lease contract under applicable law.

6. IF YOU ARE IN DEFAULT: If you are in default, Lessor may terminate this Lease, and repossess the Vehicle. In addition, you may be subject to suit and liability for the unpaid indebtedness evidenced by this Agreement.

7. AT THE END OF THE LEASE: You agree to return the Vehicle in good condition, at the end of the Lease to the address Lessor gives you and you will owe no other fees or payments, unless you desire to buy the Vehicle. You have the option to purchase the Vehicle only at the end of the Lease. The purchase price shall be established as the fair market value of the Vehicle at the end of the term of the Lease.

8. PROHIBITION OF TRANSFER OF LESSEE'S INTEREST: You will not sublease, rent assign, grant a security interest in or otherwise transfer your interest under this Lease in a way that affects your possession or use of the Vehicle or any other right in the Vehicle, nor will you attempt to transfer any other right or interest under this Lease or in the Vehicle. However, Lessor, upon request, may give prior written consent to a transfer.

9. INDEMNITY: You will protect Lessor, and anyone to whom Lessor assigns this Lease, from all losses, damages, injuries, claims, demands, and expenses arising out of the condition, maintenance, use, or operation of the Vehicle. In addition, you agree to indemnify and hold Lessor and its assigns harmless from any and all losses, damages, injuries, claims, demands, and expenses.

10. DELIVERY RECEIPT: By signing this Lease, you agree that **(i)** You received and

examined the Vehicle described in this Lease, **(ii)** the Vehicle is as described in this Lease, and **(iii)** the Vehicle is in good working order and condition.

11. ENTIRE AGREEMENT: This Lease contains the entire Agreement between You and Lessor. There are no other agreements between you and Lessor, except those written in this Lease. No course of performance will be used to determine the meaning of this Lease or to show a change to this Lease and no changes to this Lease will be valid unless committed to writing and signed by You and Lessor.

12. ADDITIONAL CONDITIONS: _____

_____

_____

13. WARRANT: The undersigned warrants that they fully understand their legal rights and obligations in connection herewith and that having understood the obligations detailed herein, has without any reservation, executed this instrument on this the _____ Day of _____ 20___.

SIGNATURES

LEESEE Name: _____ Signature: _____

LEESOR Name: _____ Signature: _____

Date

Internal Revenue Service
The address of your local IRS
Office for filing 1120 corporate tax returns

Reference: **Zero Income 1120 Tax Return**

Dear Sir or Madam

I am an officer of the above named corporation. This last filing period our company had no income (***or put has yet to start business***). For this reason, we did not file an 1120 tax return.

If this is not acceptable, please advise us that a zero income 1120 is required and we shall gladly prepare one and forward it to your office forthwith.

Thank you for your kind assistance regarding this matter.

Respectfully

Your name
Title

Asset Protection Services of America

**Corporation
Documents**

RESOLUTION OF
(Replace This With The Name Of Your Corp)
A (Name of State) CORPORATION
TO
ACQUIRE ASSETS OF A BUSINESS

The Secretary announced that pursuant to the Articles of Incorporation and/or Bylaws of the above named Corporation, a special meeting of the Directors was held on the _____ day of _____, 20___ at _____ o'clock ___M. The chairman then declared that the meeting was to be held in compliance with applicable statutes.

WHEREAS, it is in the best interests of the Corporation to acquire the assets of the following entity as a going concern: _____*(put in the business name)*.

It is hereby **RESOLVED**, that the Corporation execute an agreement to purchase the business assets of the above-stated Corporation as per the purchase agreement attached hereto; and it is further **RESOLVED**, that the Director or other Officer of the Corporation named: _____ be and is hereby authorized to execute such further documents and undertake such other acts as are reasonably required to carry out and conclude said transaction to purchase assets.

_____   _____
Director   Director

CERTIFICATION OF CORPORATE SECRETARY

I the undersigned, certify that I am the duly appointed Secretary of the above named Corporation and that the forgoing Resolution is a true and accurate copy of a Resolution duly adopted at a meeting of the Shareholders thereof, convened and held in accordance with the Bylaws of said Corporation and that the Resolution is now in full force and effect.

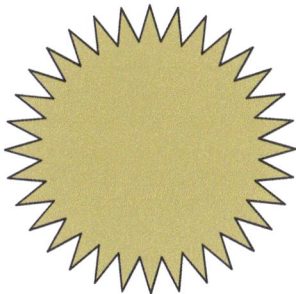

IN WITNESS THEREOF, I have affixed my name as Secretary of the above named Corporation and have attached the seal of said Corporation to this Resolution.

Dated _____ 20___

_____
Corporate Secretary

AMENDMENT TO
ARTICLES OF INCORPORATION AND/OR BYLAWS
FOR
(Replace This With The Name Of Your Corp)
A *(Name of State)* CORPORATION

There was presented to the Shareholders an amendment to the _____ Articles of Incorporation / _____ Bylaws for the Corporation. After consideration by the Shareholders of the Corporation, it was **RESOLVED,** that the following amendment be made:

_____

_____

_____

_____

_____

_____

The Secretary shall amend the document, file the document with the proper State agencies, if necessary, and distribute the amended document to the Shareholders of the Corporation.

_____   _____

Shareholders   Shareholders

_____   _____

Shareholders   Shareholders

_____   _____

Shareholders   Shareholders

WE, the undersigned, being all of the Directors of the Corporation, hereby agree and consent that the annual meeting of Board of Directors of the Corporation be held on the date and time and at the place designated hereunder, and do hereby waive all notice whatsoever of such meeting and of any adjournment or adjournments thereof.

We do further agree and consent that any and all lawful business may be transacted at such meeting or at any adjournment or adjournments thereof as may be deemed advisable by the Directors present thereat. Any business transacted at such meeting or at any adjournment or adjournments thereof shall be as valid and legal and of the same force and effect as if such meeting or adjourned meeting were held after notice.

Place of Meeting: _____

Date of Meeting: _____ Time of Meeting: _____

Purpose of Meeting: _____

Dated: _____

Shareholder: _____

Shareholder: _____

CERTIFICATION OF CORPORATE SECRETARY

I the undersigned, certify that I am the duly appointed Secretary of the above named Corporation and that the forgoing Resolution is a true and accurate copy of a Resolution duly adopted at a meeting of the Shareholders thereof, convened and held in accordance with the Bylaws of said Corporation and that the Resolution is now in full force and effect.

IN WITNESS THEREOF, I have affixed my name as Secretary of the above named Corporation and have attached the seal of said Corporation to this Resolution.

Dated _____ 20___

_____
Corporate Secretary

MINUTES OF THE ANNUAL MEETING OF
THE BOARD OF DIRECTORS
OF
(Replace This With The Name Of Your Corp)
A *(Name of State)* CORPORATION

The annual meeting of the Board of Directors immediately followed the annual meeting of the Shareholders. All the Directors of the Corporation were present. The meeting was then called to order by _____ as Chairman and that _____ acted in the capacity of the Secretary.

The Chairman noted that it was in order to consider electing officers for the ensuing year. Upon nominations duly made and seconded, the following were unanimously elected officers of the Corporation, to serve for the ensuing year and until their successors are elected and qualified:

President: _____

Vice-President: _____

Secretary: _____

Treasurer: _____

There being no further business to come before the meeting, upon motion duly made, seconded and unanimously carried, it was adjourned.

Secretary: _____

Attested to by Board of Directors.

Director: _____

Director: _____

Director: _____

WAIVER OF NOTICE OF ANNUAL MEETING
OF SHAREHOLDERS
OF
(Replace This With The Name Of Your Corp)
A *(Name of State)* CORPORATION

WE, the undersigned, being all of the Shareholders of the Corporation, hereby agree and consent that the annual meeting of Shareholders of the Corporation be held on the date and time and at the place designated hereunder, and do hereby waive all notice whatsoever of such meeting and of any adjournment or adjournments thereof.

We do agree and consent that any and all lawful business may be transacted at such meeting or at any adjournment or adjournments thereof as may be deemed advisable by the Directors present thereat. Any business transacted at such meeting or at any adjournment or adjournments thereof shall be as valid and legal and of the same force and effect as if such meeting or adjourned meeting were held after notice.

Place of Meeting: _____

Date of Meeting: _____ Time of Meeting: _____

Purpose of Meeting: _____

Dated: _____

Shareholder: _____

Shareholder: _____

CERTIFICATION OF CORPORATE SECRETARY

I the undersigned, certify that I am the duly appointed Secretary of the above named Corporation and that the forgoing Resolution is a true and accurate copy of a Resolution duly adopted at a meeting of the Shareholders thereof, convened and held in accordance with the Bylaws of said Corporation and that the Resolution is now in full force and effect.

IN WITNESS THEREOF, I have affixed my name as Secretary of the above named Corporation and have attached the seal of said Corporation to this Resolution.

Dated _____ 20____

_____
Corporate Secretary

MINUTES OF THE
ANNUAL MEETING OF THE SHAREHOLDERS
OF
(Replace This With The Name Of Your Corp)
A *(Name of State)* CORPORATION

The annual meeting of Shareholders of the above mentioned Corporation was held on the date and at the time and place set forth in the written Waiver of Notice signed by the Shareholders, fixing such time and place, and prefixed to the minutes of this meeting. There were present the following Shareholders:

Shareholders   **Number of Shares**

Signature: _____ Printed Name: _____   _____

Signature: _____ Printed Name: _____   _____

The meeting was then called to order by _____ as Chairman and that _____ acted in the capacity of the Secretary. The Chairman then stated that all outstanding shares of the Corporation were represented. The President presented his annual report and, after discussion, the report was accepted and ordered filed with the Secretary.

The Chairman noted that it was in order to consider electing a Board of Directors for the ensuing year. Upon nominations duly made, seconded and unanimously carried, the following persons were elected as Directors of the Corporation, to serve for a period of one year and until such time as their successors are elected and qualify.

CERTIFICATION OF CORPORATE SECRETARY

I the undersigned, certify that I am the duly appointed Secretary of the above named Corporation and that the forgoing Resolution is a true and accurate copy of a Resolution duly adopted at a meeting of the Shareholders thereof, convened and held in accordance with the Bylaws of said Corporation and that the Resolution is now in full force and effect.

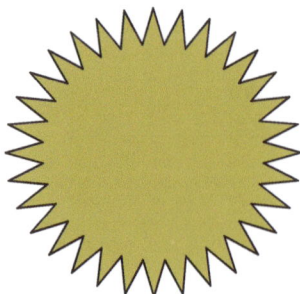

IN WITNESS THEREOF, I have affixed my name as Secretary of the above named Corporation and have attached the seal of said Corporation to this Resolution.

Dated _____ 20___

_____
Corporate Secretary

RESOLUTION OF
(Replace This With The Name Of Your Corp)
A *(Name of State)* CORPORATION
FOR
BILL OF SALE & AGREEMENT

The Secretary announced that pursuant to the Articles of Incorporation and/or Bylaws of the above named Corporation, a special meeting of the Directors was held on the _____ day of _____, 20____ at _____ o'clock ___M. The chairman then declared that the meeting was to be held in compliance with applicable statutes.

This is an agreement between the undersigned (referred to as "Transferor") and the above named Corporation (referred to as "Corporation").

In return for the issuance of _____ shares of stock of the Corporation, Transferor sells assigns and transfers to the Corporation all right, title and interest in the property and assets shown on **ATTACHMENT "A"** which must be attached hereto and thereby made a part hereof.

In return for the transfer of said property, the Corporation agrees to assume, pay and discharge all debts, duties and obligations that exist as of the date of transfer to this Corporation. Further, the Corporation agrees to indemnify and hold Transferor free from any liability for any such debts, duties and obligations, suits, actions, or legal proceedings brought to enforce or collect such debt, duty or obligation.

In addition, appoints the Corporation to do all things allowed by law to demand, receive, and collect for itself any debt or obligation now owing and authorizes it to recover and collect any such debt or obligation and to use the name(s) of Transferor in such manner as it considers necessary to collect and recover such debts or obligations

On this the _____ day of _____ 20____ we the undersigned set our hands and executed this agreement.

TRANSFEROR Signature: _____

Printed Name: _____

CORPORATION Signature: _____

Printed Name: _____

Title: _____

CERTIFICATION OF CORPORATE SECRETARY

I the undersigned, certify that I am the duly appointed Secretary of the above named Corporation and that the forgoing Resolution is a true and accurate copy of a Resolution duly adopted at a meeting of the Shareholders thereof, convened and held in accordance with the Bylaws of said Corporation and that the Resolution is now in full force and effect.

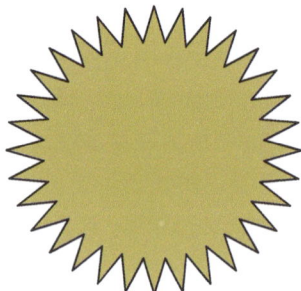

IN WITNESS THEREOF, I have affixed my name as Secretary of the above named Corporation and have attached the seal of said Corporation to this Resolution.

Dated _____ 20___

_____
Corporate Secretary

BLANK DIRECTOR'S RESOLUTION
OF
(Replace This With The Name Of Your Corp)
A *(Name of State)* CORPORATION
TO

_____

The Secretary announced that pursuant to the Articles of Incorporation and/or Bylaws of the above named Corporation, a special meeting of the Directors was held on the _____ day of _____, 20___ at _____ o'clock ___M. The chairman then declared that the meeting was to be held in compliance with applicable statutes.

The chairman of the meeting then discussed:

_____

_____

_____

On motion duly made and carried, it was **RESOLVED** and **ORDERED** that:

_____

_____

_____

CERTIFICATION OF CORPORATE SECRETARY

I the undersigned, certify that I am the duly appointed Secretary of the above named Corporation and that the forgoing Resolution is a true and accurate copy of a Resolution duly adopted at a meeting of the Shareholders thereof, convened and held in accordance with the Bylaws of said Corporation and that the Resolution is now in full force and effect.

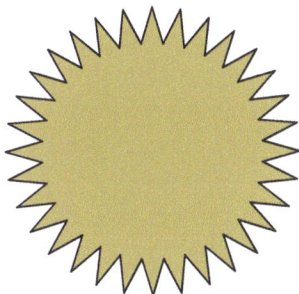

IN WITNESS THEREOF, I have affixed my name as Secretary of the above named Corporation and have attached the seal of said Corporation to this Resolution.

Dated _____ 20___

_____

Corporate Secretary

_____

RESOLVED that the above named Corporation elects _____
_____, for _____,
purposes. The officers of the Corporation are directed to take any further action necessary for
the Corporation to obtain qualify for _____.

SHAREHOLDERS' CONSENT

The undersigned Shareholders being all of the Shareholders of the above Corporation hereby
consents to the election of the Corporation to obtain qualify for _____ purposes.

Name & Address of Shareholder	Shares Owned	Date Acquired
1.) _____	_____	____ / _____ / 20____
Signed: _____	Date: _____	
2.) _____	_____	____ / _____ / 20____
Signed: _____	Date: _____	

CERTIFICATION OF CORPORATE SECRETARY

I the undersigned, certify that I am the duly appointed Secretary of the above named
Corporation and that the forgoing Resolution is a true and accurate copy of a Resolution duly
adopted at a meeting of the Shareholders thereof, convened and held in accordance with the
Bylaws of said Corporation and that the Resolution is now in full force and effect.

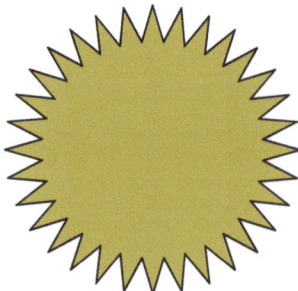

IN WITNESS THEREOF, I have affixed my name as
Secretary of the above named Corporation and have
attached the seal of said Corporation to this Resolution.

Dated _____ 20____

_____
Corporate Secretary

RESOLUTION OF
(Replace This With The Name Of Your Corp)
A *(Name of State)* CORPORATION
FOR
BORROWING CAPITAL

The Secretary announced that pursuant to the Articles of Incorporation and/or Bylaws of the above named Corporation, a special meeting of the Directors was held on the _____ day of _____, 20____ at _____ o'clock ___M. The chairman then declared that the meeting was to be held in compliance with applicable statutes.

WHEREAS, the Corporation is in need of additional capital, and

WHEREAS, _____ _____, as a _____ Director / _____ Officer of the Corporation, has agreed to loan to the Corporation the sum of _____ ($_____) and

WHEREAS, such borrowing appears to be advantageous to the Corporation, as it is on better terms than would be available elsewhere; be it **RESOLVED** and **ORDERED**, that the Corporation borrow the sum of _____ ($_____) from the above named _____ Director / _____ Officer, and that said sum be repaid in or within _____ years with interest thereon at _____ _____ (____%) on the unpaid balance, all as more fully set forth in a promissory note and collateral loan documents that when executed, must be placed in the minutes of this Corporation.

CERTIFICATION OF CORPORATE SECRETARY

I the undersigned, certify that I am the duly appointed Secretary of the above named Corporation and that the forgoing Resolution is a true and accurate copy of a Resolution duly adopted at a meeting of the Shareholders thereof, convened and held in accordance with the Bylaws of said Corporation and that the Resolution is now in full force and effect.

IN WITNESS THEREOF, I have affixed my name as Secretary of the above named Corporation and have attached the seal of said Corporation to this Resolution.

Dated _____ 20____

_____
Corporate Secretary

BORROWING CAPITAL

THIS LOAN AGREEMENT is entered into this _____ day of _____ 20___, by and between _____,
whose address is _____
_____ (hereinafter referred to as "Lender"),
and_____,
whose address is _____
_____ (hereinafter referred to as "Borrower"),
who agree as follows:

1. LOAN AMOUNT (PRINCIPAL): Lender agrees to loan Borrower the sum of _____
($_____) Dollars pursuant to the terms and conditions contained in this Agreement.

1.1. INCREASES IN LOAN AMOUNT (PRINCIPAL): Lender agrees that from time to time, he/she/it MAY make additional loans to Borrower, under the terms and conditions of this Agreement. Therefore, in the interest of the ease of officiating and tracking same, the parties hereby agree that any such increase in the loan amount, shall be deemed an amendment to this agreement, and shall be added to the then existing amount (a new loan agreement shall not be required for each loan), and thereby handled as though the additional loan(s) were part and parcel of the original loan for which this Agreement was executed.

2. CALL DATE: The principal amount (above) of this loan, shall be due and repayable
_____ one (1) year;
_____ two (2) years;
_____ three (3) years;
_____ four (4) years;
_____ five (5) years;
_____ as funds are available from Borrower;
_____ when called by lender; or
_____ Other: _____;
from the date first written above.

2.1. IF REPAYMENT IS BY "AS FUNDS ARE AVAILABLE": Should the principal amount be repaid as funds are available, said payments shall be shown on a separate ledger which shall reflect the amount of the principal and the amount of each payment.

3. INTEREST: The interest on this loan shall be established at _____ (____%) per annum, and shall be due and payable on a _____ monthly, _____ quarterly, _____ annual basis, and shall commence on the _____ Day of _____, 20___.

4. ATTORNEY AND OTHER LEGAL FEES: Both parties hereby agree that in the event that either party commences an action at law or in equity against the other to enforce any of the terms, conditions, covenants, promises or provisions of this Agreement by reason of a breach or default hereunder, the party prevailing in any such action or proceedings, shall be entitled to, and receive all reasonable attorney's fees and other such costs from the other party. In the event a judgment is secured by such prevailing party, all such fees shall be included in said judgment and shall be set by the court and not a jury.

5. INVALIDITY OF PARTICULAR PROVISION(S): In the event that any portion of this Agreement shall, for any reason, be deemed to be invalid or unenforceable, the remaining portions of this Agreement shall be fully effective, valid and enforceable.

6. VENUE, SUCCESSOR AND ASSIGNS: Both parties hereby agree that the venue of all the terms, Conditions and provisions of this Agreement shall be the State of _____, and shall inure to the benefit of, and be binding upon heirs, successors and assigns of the parties hereto.

7. ENTIRE AGREEMENT: This Agreement contains the entire agreement between the parties hereto. No modifications, amendments or changes in any of the terms, Conditions or provisions hereof shall be valid unless signed by both parties and attached hereto as an amendment.

8. NOTICES: All notices and other communications under this Agreement, must be in writing, and must be mailed by registered or certified mail, or delivered by hand to the party to whom such notice is required to be given. If mailed, any such notice shall be considered to have been given three (3) business days after it was mailed, as evidenced by the postmark. If delivered by hand, when receive by the party, or their designated representative, as evidenced by a written and dated receipt of the receiving party. The mailing address for notice to either party, shall be the address shown herein.

IN WITNESS WHEREOF, the parties have executed this Agreement as of the day first written above.

BORROWER

Signed: _____

Title: _____

Printed Name: _____

LENDER

Signed: _____

Title: _____

Printed Name: _____

RESOLUTION OF
(Replace This With The Name Of Your Corp)
A *(Name of State)* CORPORATION
TO
BORROW ON ACCOUNTS RECEIVABLE, EQUIPMENT, INVENTORY

The Secretary announced that pursuant to the Articles of Incorporation and/or Bylaws of the above named Corporation, a special meeting of the Directors was held on the _____ day of _____, 20___ at _____ o'clock __M. The chairman then declared that the meeting was to be held in compliance with applicable statutes.

RESOLVED and **ORDERED**, that the President of this Corporation, is hereby authorized and directed to borrow the sum of _____ ($_____) Dollars from any entity or individual on the terms set out in a contract or Promissory Note which when executed must be placed in the minutes of this meeting and to execute a mortgage in favor of the Lender covering the accounts receivable, equipment, fixtures, furniture, inventory or merchandise set out in a Schedule attached to the minutes of this meeting.

Therefore, it is **FURTHER RESOLVED** and **ORDERED**, that the President of the Corporation is hereby authorized and directed to provide for creditors of the Corporation all notices required by law to be given to the creditors of the Corporation, and to do everything else that may be necessary to complete the authorized transaction.

CERTIFICATION OF CORPORATE SECRETARY

I the undersigned, certify that I am the duly appointed Secretary of the above named Corporation and that the forgoing Resolution is a true and accurate copy of a Resolution duly adopted at a meeting of the Shareholders thereof, convened and held in accordance with the Bylaws of said Corporation and that the Resolution is now in full force and effect.

IN WITNESS THEREOF, I have affixed my name as Secretary of the above named Corporation and have attached the seal of said Corporation to this Resolution.

Dated _____ 20___

_____
Corporate Secretary

MINUTES OF A SPECIAL MEETING
OF THE DIRECTORS OF
(Replace This With The Name Of Your Corp)
A *(Name of State)* CORPORATION
FOR
DEMISE OR INCAPACITATION OF OFFICERS

The Secretary announced that pursuant to the Articles of Incorporation and/or Bylaws of the above named Corporation, a special meeting of the Directors was held on the _____ day of _____, 20____ at _____ o'clock ___M. The chairman then declared that the meeting was to be held in compliance with applicable statutes.

The chairman of the meeting then discussed electing assistant officers who shall immediately replace their respective elected officers in case of the demise or incapacitation of any or all of the current officers of this Corporation pursuant to the Bylaws of this Corporation. On motion duly made and carried, it was **RESOLVED** and **ORDERED** that the following individuals be elected and each has accepted their respective offices at the meeting:

ASSISTANT PRESIDENT: _____

ASSISTANT SECRETARY: _____

ASSISTANT TREASURER: _____

The chairman of the meeting then discussed electing substitute signatories on any and all corporate bank accounts and merchant accounts for this Corporation in case of the demise or incapacitation of any or all of the current signatories of this Corporation. On motion duly made and carried, it was; **RESOLVED** and **ORDERED** that the following individual be elected as substitute signatories on any and all Corporation bank accounts and merchant accounts for this Corporation in case of the demise or incapacitation of any or all of the current signatories of this Corporation and each has accepted their respective offices at the meeting:

_____   _____
Printed Name   Signature

_____   _____
Printed Name   Signature

_____   _____
Printed Name   Signature

The chairman of the meeting then discussed electing substitute signatories on any and all Corporate bank accounts and merchant accounts for this Corporation in case of the demise or incapacitation of any or all of the current signatories of this Corporation.

On motion duly made and carried, it was **RESOLVED** and **ORDERED** that the following individuals be elected as substitute signatories on any and all Corporate bank accounts and merchant accounts for this Corporation in case of the demise or incapacitation of any or all of the current signatories of this Corporation and each has accepted their respective offices at the meeting:

_____   _____
Printed Name   Signature

_____   _____
Printed Name   Signature

CERTIFICATION OF CORPORATE SECRETARY

I the undersigned, certify that I am the duly appointed Secretary of the above named Corporation and that the forgoing Resolution is a true and accurate copy of a Resolution duly adopted at a meeting of the Shareholders thereof, convened and held in accordance with the Bylaws of said Corporation and that the Resolution is now in full force and effect.

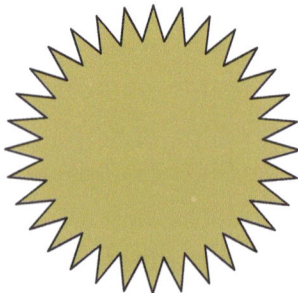

IN WITNESS THEREOF, I have affixed my name as Secretary of the above named Corporation and have attached the seal of said Corporation to this Resolution.

Dated _____ 20____

_____
Corporate Secretary

RESOLUTION OF
(Replace This With The Name Of Your Corp)
A (Name of State) CORPORATION
FOR
DISSOLUTION OF CORPORATION

The Secretary announced that pursuant to the Articles of Incorporation and/or Bylaws of the above named Corporation, a special meeting of the Directors was held on the _____ day of _____, 20____ at _____ o'clock ___M. The chairman then declared that the meeting was to be held in compliance with applicable statutes.

RESOLVED that _____ shall dissolve forthwith, and it is:

FURTHER RESOLVED and **ORDERED**, that the President of the Corporation is hereby authorized and directed to file the necessary Certificate of Dissolution of this Corporation with Secretary of State in accordance with the laws of the State of _____.

CERTIFICATION OF CORPORATE SECRETARY

I the undersigned, certify that I am the duly appointed Secretary of the above named Corporation and that the forgoing Resolution is a true and accurate copy of a Resolution duly adopted at a meeting of the Shareholders thereof, convened and held in accordance with the Bylaws of said Corporation and that the Resolution is now in full force and effect.

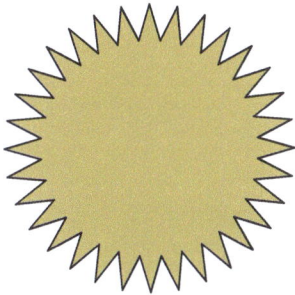

IN WITNESS THEREOF, I have affixed my name as Secretary of the above named Corporation and have attached the seal of said Corporation to this Resolution.

Dated _____ 20____

_____
Corporate Secretary

RESOLUTION OF
(Replace This With The Name Of Your Corp)
A *(Name of State)* CORPORATION
FOR
EMPLOYEE BENEFIT PLANS

The Secretary announced that pursuant to the Articles of Incorporation and/or Bylaws of the above named Corporation, a special meeting of the Directors was held on the _____ day of _____, 20____ at _____ o'clock ___M. The chairman then declared that the meeting was to be held in compliance with applicable statutes.

WHEREAS, the Board of Directors of this Corporation considers it to be in the best interests of this Corporation to adopt the following employee benefit/incentive plans:

_____ PROFIT SHARING
_____ PENSION PLAN
_____ LIFE INSURANCE *(approved only in the event that the corporation is the beneficiary)*
_____ TERM INSURANCE *(approved only in the event that the corporation is the beneficiary)*
_____ MEDICAL AND DENTAL *(approved in the Organization minutes)*
_____ 401(K) RETIREMENT

Therefore, be it **RESOLVED** and **ORDERED**, that the Corporation adopt those plans on the above list that are checked, in accordance with acceptable programs and contracts for same.

Be it **FURTHER RESOLVED** and **ORDERED** that the President be directed to undertake such acts as are necessary to implement and administer said plans.

CERTIFICATION OF CORPORATE SECRETARY

I the undersigned, certify that I am the duly appointed Secretary of the above named Corporation and that the forgoing Resolution is a true and accurate copy of a Resolution duly adopted at a meeting of the Shareholders thereof, convened and held in accordance with the Bylaws of said Corporation and that the Resolution is now in full force and effect.

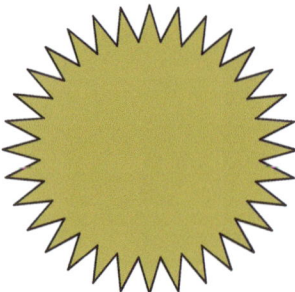

IN WITNESS THEREOF, I have affixed my name as Secretary of the above named Corporation and have attached the seal of said Corporation to this Resolution.

Dated _____ 20____

_____
Corporate Secretary

MINUTES OF A SPECIAL MEETING
OF THE BOARD OF DIRECTORS OF
(Replace This With The Name Of Your Corp)
A *(Name of State)* CORPORATION
FOR
EXCHANGE OF STOCK

The Secretary announced that pursuant to the Articles of Incorporation and/or Bylaws of the above named Corporation, a special meeting of the Directors was held on the _____ day of _____, 20____ at _____ o'clock ___M. The chairman then declared that the meeting was to be held in compliance with applicable statutes.

The following proposal by _____ for exchanging the stock of this Corporation was presented by the Chairman who indicated that this Corporation should exchange common stock of this Corporation in exchange for:

_____ a promissory note in the amount of _____ ($_____),

_____ cash in the amount of _____ ($_____),

_____ services rendered or to be rendered valued at _____ ($_____).

Upon due consideration, the Directors determined that the consideration offered by _____ for the above stock was reasonably worth the number of shares for which same was offered and that it was in the best interest of the Corporation to accept said exchange. Upon motion duly made, seconded and carried, it was; **RESOLVED** and **ORDERED** that this Corporation should exchange _____ (_____) shares of the common stock of this Corporation to _____ in order to facilitate the exchange contemplated herein.

CERTIFICATION OF CORPORATE SECRETARY

I the undersigned, certify that I am the duly appointed Secretary of the above named Corporation and that the forgoing Resolution is a true and accurate copy of a Resolution duly adopted at a meeting of the Shareholders thereof, convened and held in accordance with the Bylaws of said Corporation and that the Resolution is now in full force and effect.

IN WITNESS THEREOF, I have affixed my name as Secretary of the above named Corporation and have attached the seal of said Corporation to this Resolution.

Dated _____ 20____

_____
Corporate Secretary

RESOLUTION OF
(Replace This With The Name Of Your Corp)
A *(Name of State)* CORPORATION
FOR
LOANING FUNDS TO OFFICER/DIRECTOR

The Secretary announced that pursuant to the Articles of Incorporation and/or Bylaws of the above named Corporation, a special meeting of the Directors was held on the _____ day of _____, 20____ at _____ o'clock ___M. The chairman then declared that the meeting was to be held in compliance with applicable statutes.

WHEREAS, _____ a _____ Director / _____ Officer of this Corporation, has requested an advance and/or loan in the amount of _____ ($_____), together with interest, and

WHEREAS, the Corporation has adequate financial resources to make such a loan without impairing its growth or profitability, and that said loan is deemed reasonably secure and in the best interests of the Corporation to make, be it therefore **RESOLVED** and **ORDERED**, that the Corporation shall issue a loan to _____ in the amount of _____ ($_____), to be repaid within _____ months with interest of _____ (_____%) on the unpaid balance, and that the borrower execute a promissory note evidencing said indebtedness to the Corporation.

CERTIFICATION OF CORPORATE SECRETARY

I the undersigned, certify that I am the duly appointed Secretary of the above named Corporation and that the forgoing Resolution is a true and accurate copy of a Resolution duly adopted at a meeting of the Shareholders thereof, convened and held in accordance with the Bylaws of said Corporation and that the Resolution is now in full force and effect.

IN WITNESS THEREOF, I have affixed my name as Secretary of the above named Corporation and have attached the seal of said Corporation to this Resolution.

Dated _____ 20____

_____
Corporate Secretary

THIS GENERAL LOAN AGREEMENT is entered into this _____ day of _____ 20___, by and between _____, whose address is _____ _____ (*hereinafter referred to as "Lender"*), and _____, whose address is _____ _____ (*hereinafter referred to as "Borrower"*), who agree as follows:

1. LOAN AMOUNT (PRINCIPAL): Lender agrees to loan Borrower the sum of _____ _____ ($_____) Dollars pursuant to the terms and conditions contained in this Agreement.

1.1. INCREASES IN LOAN AMOUNT (PRINCIPAL): Lender agrees that from time to time, he/she/it MAY make additional loans to Borrower, under the terms and conditions of this Agreement. Therefore, in the interest of the ease of officiating and tracking same, the parties hereby agree that any such increase in the loan amount, shall be deemed an amendment to this agreement, and shall be added to the then existing amount (a new loan agreement shall not be required for each loan), and thereby handled as though the additional loan(s) were part and parcel of the original loan for which this Agreement was executed.

2. CALL DATE: The principal amount (above) of this loan, shall be due and repayable

_____ one (1) year;
_____ two (2) years;
_____ three (3) years;
_____ four (4) years;
_____ five (5) years;
_____ as funds are available from Borrower;
_____ when called by lender; or
_____ Other: _____;

from the date first written above.

3. INTEREST: The interest on this loan shall be established at _____ (____%) per annum, and shall be due and payable on a _____ monthly, _____ quarterly, _____ annual basis, and shall commence on the _____ Day of _____, 20___.

4. ATTORNEY AND OTHER LEGAL FEES: Both parties hereby agree that in the event that either party commences an action at law or in equity against the other to enforce any of the terms, conditions, covenants, promises or provisions of this Agreement by reason of a breach or default hereunder, the party prevailing in any such action or proceedings, shall be entitled to, and receive all reasonable attorney's fees and other such costs from the other party. In the event a judgment is secured by such prevailing party, all such fees shall be included in said judgment and shall be set by the court and not a jury.

5. INVALIDITY OF PARTICULAR PROVISION(S): In the event that any portion of this Agreement shall, for any reason, be deemed to be invalid or unenforceable, the remaining portions of this Agreement shall be fully effective, valid and enforceable.

6. VENUE, SUCCESSOR AND ASSIGNS: Both parties hereby agree that the venue of all the terms, Conditions and provisions of this Agreement shall be the State of _____, and shall inure to the benefit of, and be binding upon heirs, successors and assigns of the parties hereto.

7. ENTIRE AGREEMENT: This Agreement contains the entire agreement between the parties hereto. No modifications, amendments or changes in any of the terms, Conditions or provisions hereof shall be valid unless signed by both parties and attached hereto as an amendment.

8. NOTICES: All notices and other communications under this Agreement, must be in writing, and must be mailed by registered or certified mail, or delivered by hand to the party to whom such notice is required to be given. If mailed, any such notice shall be considered to have been given three (3) business days after it was mailed, as evidenced by the postmark. If delivered by hand, when receive by the party, or their designated representative, as evidenced by a written and dated receipt of the receiving party. The mailing address for notice to either party shall be the address shown herein.

IN WITNESS WHEREOF, the parties have executed this Agreement as of the day first written above.

BORROWER

Signed: _____

Title: _____

Printed Name: _____

LENDER

Signed: _____

Title: _____

Printed Name: _____

MINUTES OF SPECIAL MEETING OF
THE BOARD OF DIRECTORS OF
(Replace This With The Name Of Your Corp)
A *(Name of State)* CORPORATION
FOR
MANAGING MEMBER OF LLC

The Secretary announced that pursuant to the Articles of Incorporation and/or Bylaws of the above named Corporation, a special meeting of the Directors was held on the _____ day of _____, 20___ at _____ o'clock ___M. The chairman then declared that the meeting was to be held in compliance with applicable statutes.

The Chairman reported that a Limited Liability Company (hereinafter LLC) named (**put in the name of the LLC**) desires to contract this Corporation to act in the capacity of the managing member of said LLC pursuant to a **Management Service Agreement** attached hereto and thereby made a part hereof.

RESOLVED that this Corporation shall undertake the responsibility of the managing member of (*put in the name of the LLC*) and for doing so shall be compensated as follows:

_____

_____

There being no further business requiring Board of Director action or consideration, On a motion duly made, seconded and carried, the meeting was adjourned.

CERTIFICATION OF CORPORATE SECRETARY

I the undersigned, certify that I am the duly appointed Secretary of the above named Corporation and that the forgoing Resolution is a true and accurate copy of a Resolution duly adopted at a meeting of the Shareholders thereof, convened and held in accordance with the Bylaws of said Corporation and that the Resolution is now in full force and effect.

IN WITNESS THEREOF, I have affixed my name as Secretary of the above named Corporation and have attached the seal of said Corporation to this Resolution.

Dated _____ 20___

_____

Corporate Secretary

RESOLUTION OF
(Replace This With The Name Of Your Corp)
A *(Name of State)* CORPORATION
TO
PURCHASE EQUIPMENT

The Secretary announced that pursuant to the Articles of Incorporation and/or Bylaws of the above named Corporation, a special meeting of the Directors was held on the _____ day of _____, 20___ at _____ o'clock ___M. The chairman then declared that the meeting was to be held in compliance with applicable statutes.

WHEREAS, certain equipment is necessary for the operation of the business, therefore be it **RESOLVED** and **ORDERED**, that this Corporation shall purchase the following equipment:

Description: _____

Model Number _____

Purchase From: _____

Purchase price: $_____

To be paid in: _____ Cash _____ Credit _____ Other: _____

CERTIFICATION OF CORPORATE SECRETARY

I the undersigned, certify that I am the duly appointed Secretary of the above named Corporation and that the forgoing Resolution is a true and accurate copy of a Resolution duly adopted at a meeting of the Shareholders thereof, convened and held in accordance with the Bylaws of said Corporation and that the Resolution is now in full force and effect.

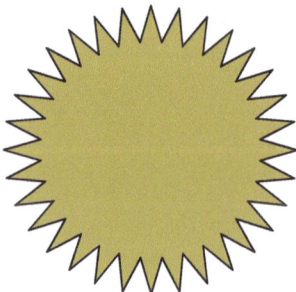

IN WITNESS THEREOF, I have affixed my name as Secretary of the above named Corporation and have attached the seal of said Corporation to this Resolution.

Dated _____ 20___

_____
Corporate Secretary

RESOLUTION OF
(Replace This With The Name Of Your Corp)
A *(Name of State)* CORPORATION
TO
PURCHASE MOTOR VEHICLES

The Secretary announced that pursuant to the Articles of Incorporation and/or Bylaws of the above named Corporation, a special meeting of the Directors was held on the _____ day of _____, 20____ at _____ o'clock ___M. The chairman then declared that the meeting was to be held in compliance with applicable statutes.

WHEREAS, motor vehicles are necessary for the operation of the business, therefore be it **RESOLVED** and **ORDERED**, that this Corporation shall purchase the motor vehicle(s) described as:

Year, Make and Model: _____

License Number _____

V.I.N. _____

Purchase From: _____

Purchase price of: $_____

To be paid in: _____ Cash _____ Credit _____ Other: _____

CERTIFICATION OF CORPORATE SECRETARY

I the undersigned, certify that I am the duly appointed Secretary of the above named Corporation and that the forgoing Resolution is a true and accurate copy of a Resolution duly adopted at a meeting of the Shareholders thereof, convened and held in accordance with the Bylaws of said Corporation and that the Resolution is now in full force and effect.

IN WITNESS THEREOF, I have affixed my name as Secretary of the above named Corporation and have attached the seal of said Corporation to this Resolution.

Dated _____ 20____

_____
Corporate Secretary

RESOLUTION OF
(Replace This With The Name Of Your Corp)
A (Name of State) CORPORATION
TO
PURCHASE REAL PROPERTY

The Secretary announced that pursuant to the Articles of Incorporation and/or Bylaws of the above named Corporation, a special meeting of the Directors was held on the _____ day of _____, 20___ at _____ o'clock __M. The chairman then declared that the meeting was to be held in compliance with applicable statutes.

WHEREAS, the Corporation has decided to purchase various parcels of real estate under the terms of the attached **Real Estate Purchase Services Agreement**.

Therefore, be it: **RESOLVED** and **ORDERED**, that the Corporation purchase and acquire said real estate as set forth in the Real Estate Purchase Services Agreement as annexed hereto and that the named Authorized Signatory shall be authorized to represent this Corporation as the signatory for any and all documentary requirements pertaining thereto.

There being no further business requiring Board of Director action or consideration, and on a motion duly made, seconded and carried, the meeting was adjourned.

CERTIFICATION OF CORPORATE SECRETARY

I the undersigned, certify that I am the duly appointed Secretary of the above named Corporation and that the forgoing Resolution is a true and accurate copy of a Resolution duly adopted at a meeting of the Shareholders thereof, convened and held in accordance with the Bylaws of said Corporation and that the Resolution is now in full force and effect.

IN WITNESS THEREOF, I have affixed my name as Secretary of the above named Corporation and have attached the seal of said Corporation to this Resolution.

Dated _____ 20___

_____
Corporate Secretary

RESOLUTION OF
(Replace This With The Name Of Your Corp)
A *(Name of State)* CORPORATION
ESTABLISHING THE AUTHORIZED SIGNATORY FOR THE
PURCHASE AND/OR SALE OF REAL PROPERTY

The Secretary announced that pursuant to the Articles of Incorporation and/or Bylaws of the above named Corporation, a special meeting of the Directors was held on the _____ day of _____, 20___ at _____ o'clock ___M. The chairman then declared that the meeting was to be held in compliance with applicable statutes.

　　　The chairman of the meeting then discussed granting full signatory authority to the named Authorized Signatory to sign any and all banking documents or instruments, contracts and/or any other documents as needed on behalf of this Corporation.

On motion duly made and carried, it was, **RESOLVED** and **ORDERED** that the named Authorized Signatory be henceforth granted the full signatory authority and power to grant, bargain, convey, sell, acquire or purchase; to sign promissory notes, mortgages or deeds of trust encumbering the property of this corporation; to contract for the sale, conveyance, acquisition or purchase of any and all property belonging to this Corporation; to execute escrow instructions, trust agreements, agreements for sale, deeds or other conveyances of land, bills of sale, construction contracts, leases, subordinate agreements subordinating any lien, encumbrance or other right in real or personal property to any other lien or encumbrance or other contracts and/or instrument(s) necessary to effect such sale, conveyance, exchange, acquisition or purchase and to give warrantees to the purchasers thereof; to execute any and all documents deemed necessary without the attestation of the Board of Directors or affixing of the Corporation seal thereto and upon execution of such instruments by the named Authorized Signatory, such documents so executed shall be valid and binding without further act or specific resolution of the Board of Directors.

CERTIFICATION OF CORPORATE SECRETARY

I the undersigned, certify that I am the duly appointed Secretary of the above named Corporation and that the forgoing Resolution is a true and accurate copy of a Resolution duly adopted at a meeting of the Shareholders thereof, convened and held in accordance with the Bylaws of said Corporation and that the Resolution is now in full force and effect.

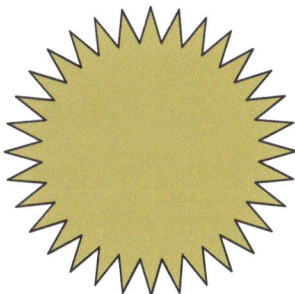

IN WITNESS THEREOF, I have affixed my name as Secretary of the above named Corporation and have attached the seal of said Corporation to this Resolution.

Dated _____ 20___

_____
Corporate Secretary

MINUTES OF A SPECIAL MEETING
OF THE DIRECTORS OF
(Replace This With The Name Of Your Corp)
A *(Name of State)* CORPORATION
TO
RECEIVE CORPORATE INCOME

The Secretary announced that pursuant to the Articles of Incorporation and/or Bylaws of the above named Corporation, a special meeting of the Directors was held on the _____ day of _____, 20___ at _____ o'clock ___M. The chairman then declared that the meeting was to be held in compliance with applicable statutes.

The chairman of the meeting then discussed having one or more of the corporate officers/ directors of the above named Corporation temporally receive incoming corporate funds into their personal bank accounts to facilitate the needs of the Corporation due to the fact that the Corporation has yet to be able to open a corporate bank account.

On motion duly made and carried, it was **RESOLVED** and **ORDERED** that the following individual will be authorized to temporally receive corporate funds in their personal name deposited into their personal bank account providing that as soon as the corporate bank account is opened, said funds so received are to be held in trust for the Corporation and transferred in total to the corporate bank account when the account is opened.

Notwithstanding the above, it was further **RESOLVED** and **ORDERED** that ALL corporate funds held in said personal bank account may not be used for any purpose with the exception of paying any lawful debt or expense of the Corporation while being held in trust for the Corporation.

Person Authorized To Receive & Hold the Funds: _____

Bank Name That Will Hold the Funds: _____

Bank Account Number That Will Hold the Funds:_____

CERTIFICATION OF CORPORATE SECRETARY

I the undersigned, certify that I am the duly appointed Secretary of the above named Corporation and that the forgoing Resolution is a true and accurate copy of a Resolution duly adopted at a meeting of the Shareholders thereof, convened and held in accordance with the Bylaws of said Corporation and that the Resolution is now in full force and effect.

IN WITNESS THEREOF, I have affixed my name as Secretary of the above named Corporation and have attached the seal of said Corporation to this Resolution.

Dated _____ 20____

_____
Corporate Secretary

RESOLUTION OF
(Replace This With The Name Of Your Corp)
A (Name of State) CORPORATION
TO
RENT/LEASE EQUIPMENT

The Secretary announced that pursuant to the Articles of Incorporation and/or Bylaws of the above named Corporation, a special meeting of the Directors was held on the _____ day of _____, 20___ at _____ o'clock __M. The chairman then declared that the meeting was to be held in compliance with applicable statutes.

WHEREAS, certain equipment is necessary for the operation of the business, therefore be it **RESOLVED** and **ORDERED**, that this Corporation shall rent or lease the following equipment:

Description: _____

Model Number: _____

Lease/Rent From: _____

Lease/Rental price: $_____

To be paid: _____ Day _____ Week _____ Month

_____ Other _____

CERTIFICATION OF CORPORATE SECRETARY

I the undersigned, certify that I am the duly appointed Secretary of the above named Corporation and that the forgoing Resolution is a true and accurate copy of a Resolution duly adopted at a meeting of the Shareholders thereof, convened and held in accordance with the Bylaws of said Corporation and that the Resolution is now in full force and effect.

IN WITNESS THEREOF, I have affixed my name as Secretary of the above named Corporation and have attached the seal of said Corporation to this Resolution.

Dated _____ 20___

_____
Corporate Secretary

RESOLUTION OF
(Replace This With The Name Of Your Corp)
A (Name of State) CORPORATION
TO
RENT/LEASE HOME OR OFFICE

The Secretary announced that pursuant to the Articles of Incorporation and/or Bylaws of the above named Corporation, a special meeting of the Directors was held on the _____ day of _____, 20____ at _____ o'clock ___M. The chairman then declared that the meeting was to be held in compliance with applicable statutes.

WHEREAS, it is necessary for the operation of the business of this Corporation to have an office location with living quarters in order for an officer of this Corporation to protect the property of this Corporation and to be able to undertake the business of the above named Corporation regardless of the hour day or night. Therefore be it **RESOLVED** and **ORDERED** that this Corporation shall rent or lease the following location pursuant to the attached lease agreement (in the Corporation name).

Office Location (Description): _____

Address: _____

Leased/Rented From (Land Lord): _____

Address: _____

There being no further business requiring Director action or consideration, and on a motion duly made, seconded and carried, the meeting was adjourned.

CERTIFICATION OF CORPORATE SECRETARY

I the undersigned, certify that I am the duly appointed Secretary of the above named Corporation and that the forgoing Resolution is a true and accurate copy of a Resolution duly adopted at a meeting of the Shareholders thereof, convened and held in accordance with the Bylaws of said Corporation and that the Resolution is now in full force and effect.

IN WITNESS THEREOF, I have affixed my name as Secretary of the above named Corporation and have attached the seal of said Corporation to this Resolution.

Dated _____ 20____

_____
Corporate Secretary

RESOLUTION OF
(Replace This With The Name Of Your Corp)
A *(Name of State)* CORPORATION
TO
RENT/LEASE MOTOR VEHICLES

The Secretary announced that pursuant to the Articles of Incorporation and/or Bylaws of the above named Corporation, a special meeting of the Directors was held on the _____ day of _____, 20___ at _____ o'clock __M. The chairman then declared that the meeting was to be held in compliance with applicable statutes.

WHEREAS, certain vehicles are necessary for the operation of the business, therefore be it **RESOLVED** and **ORDERED**, that this Corporation shall rent or lease the following vehicles:

Year, Make and Model: _____

License Number: _____

V.I.N. _____

Purchase From: _____

Purchase price of: $_____

To be paid in: _____ Cash _____ Credit _____ Other:_____

CERTIFICATION OF CORPORATE SECRETARY

I the undersigned, certify that I am the duly appointed Secretary of the above named Corporation and that the forgoing Resolution is a true and accurate copy of a Resolution duly adopted at a meeting of the Shareholders thereof, convened and held in accordance with the Bylaws of said Corporation and that the Resolution is now in full force and effect.

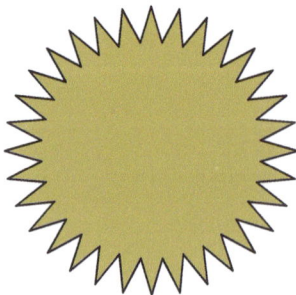

IN WITNESS THEREOF, I have affixed my name as Secretary of the above named Corporation and have attached the seal of said Corporation to this Resolution.

Dated _____ 20___

_____
Corporate Secretary

RESIGNATION OF AN
OFFICER / DIRECTOR
OF
(Replace This With The Name Of Your Corp)
A *(Name of State)* CORPORATION

On this the _____ day of _____ 20____, I, _____ do
herewith offer my resignation as an officer / director for _____.

Said resignation shall become effective from the date first stated above.

_____
Director

MINUTES OF THE MEETING OF BOARD OF DIRECTORS OF
(Replace This With The Name Of Your Corp)
A *(Name of State)* CORPORATION
FOR
RESIGNATION OF OFFICER / DIRECTOR

The Secretary announced that pursuant to the Articles of Incorporation and/or Bylaws of the above named Corporation, a special meeting of the Directors was held on the _____ day of _____, 20____ at _____ o'clock ___M. The chairman then declared that the meeting was to be held in compliance with applicable statutes.

The resignation of _____ (*copy attached*), as the officer / director for this corporation, was then read by the Secretary. On motion duly made and carried, it was; **RESOLVED** and **ORDERED** that the proposed resignation of _____ as the _____ for this Corporation be accepted as drafted. In addition, it was **RESOLVED**, that this resignation shall be effective as of the date first written above, and on that same day _____ was nominated as the new _____ and at that meeting, _____ agreed to accept said position offered.

There being no further business requiring Board of Director action or consideration, On a motion duly made, seconded and carried, the meeting was adjourned.

CERTIFICATION OF CORPORATE SECRETARY

I the undersigned, certify that I am the duly appointed Secretary of the above named Corporation and that the forgoing Resolution is a true and accurate copy of a Resolution duly adopted at a meeting of the Shareholders thereof, convened and held in accordance with the Bylaws of said Corporation and that the Resolution is now in full force and effect.

IN WITNESS THEREOF, I have affixed my name as Secretary of the above named Corporation and have attached the seal of said Corporation to this Resolution.

Dated _____ 20____

_____
Corporate Secretary

RESOLUTION OF DIRECTORS OF
(Replace This With The Name Of Your Corp)
A *(Name of State)* CORPORATION
FOR
SETTING OFFICER SALARY

The Secretary announced that pursuant to the Articles of Incorporation and/or Bylaws of the above named Corporation, a special meeting of the Directors was held on the _____ day of _____, 20____ at _____ o'clock ___M. The chairman then declared that the meeting was to be held in compliance with applicable statutes.

WHEREAS, the Corporation desires to fill the position of _____ (**put in the type of officer**) for the yearly gross salary of _____ ($_____) with all usual deductions and benefits;

It is hereby **RESOLVED**, that _____ (**put in the person's name**) be entered on the payroll records of the Corporation with salary stated above.

The salary of any Officers shall not commence until such time as the Corporation is profitable so as not to place the Corporation into financial distress by paying such salary.

_____   _____
Director   Director

CERTIFICATION OF CORPORATE SECRETARY

I the undersigned, certify that I am the duly appointed Secretary of the above named Corporation and that the forgoing Resolution is a true and accurate copy of a Resolution duly adopted at a meeting of the Shareholders thereof, convened and held in accordance with the Bylaws of said Corporation and that the Resolution is now in full force and effect.

IN WITNESS THEREOF, I have affixed my name as Secretary of the above named Corporation and have attached the seal of said Corporation to this Resolution.

Dated _____ 20____

_____
Corporate Secretary

RESOLUTION OF
THE BOARD OF DIRECTORS OF
(Replace This With The Name Of Your Corp)
A *(Name of State)* CORPORATION
FOR
SALE OF CORPORATE STOCK TO QUALIFIED INVESTORS

The Secretary announced that pursuant to the Articles of Incorporation and/or Bylaws of the above named Corporation, a special meeting of the Directors was held on the _____ day of _____, 20___ at _____ o'clock __M. The chairman then declared that the meeting was to be held in compliance with applicable statutes.

WHEREAS, the aforesaid Corporation would benefit from the sale of Corporate Stock for the development of business and marketing, be it **RESOLVED**, that the Board of Directors of the aforesaid Corporation herewith approve the issue and sale of _____ (____) shares of stock of the Corporation.

FURTHER RESOLVED, that the stock to be offered will be _____ (____) shares of stock, and that the authorized capital stock of the Corporation is _____ (____) shares, at a par value of _____ ($_____) Dollars per share.

FURTHER RESOLVED, that the Board of Directors of the aforesaid Corporation may offer for sale all or any part of the authorized capital stock of the Corporation, as deemed advisable, and that the sale price of the stock of the Corporation is _____ ($_____) dollars per share, and that all stock purchases will be for:

_____ assets (_____)   _____ cash   _____ equipment (_____)   _____ services

CERTIFICATION OF CORPORATE SECRETARY

I the undersigned, certify that I am the duly appointed Secretary of the above named Corporation and that the forgoing Resolution is a true and accurate copy of a Resolution duly adopted at a meeting of the Shareholders thereof, convened and held in accordance with the Bylaws of said Corporation and that the Resolution is now in full force and effect.

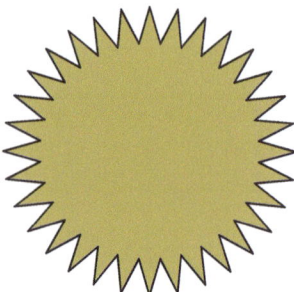

IN WITNESS THEREOF, I have affixed my name as Secretary of the above named Corporation and have attached the seal of said Corporation to this Resolution.

Dated _____ 20___

_____
Corporate Secretary

RESOLUTION OF THE BOARD OF DIRECTORS OF
(Replace This With The Name Of Your Corp)
A *(Name of State)* CORPORATION
FOR
SUBSCRIPTION AGREEMENT OF INVESTOR
FOR PURCHASE OF CORPORATE STOCK

The Secretary announced that pursuant to the Articles of Incorporation and/or Bylaws of the above named Corporation, a special meeting of the Directors was held on the _____ day of _____, 20___ at _____ o'clock ___M. The chairman then declared that the meeting was to be held in compliance with applicable statutes.

WHEREAS, certain interest parties have organized a Corporation under the Laws of the State of _____, to be known as _____ with its principal office and place of business at_____ with the State of _____, and that said Corporation has an authorized capitalization of _____ (_____) shares of Common Stock, with a _____ ($_____) dollar par value.

NOW THEREFORE, I, _____ do hereby subscribe to _____ (_____) shares of Stock of the aforesaid Corporation, and that said subscription is in full accordance with the terms and conditions as hereinafter provided:

1. Payment for the subscription of the Stock will be made at the rate of _____ ($_____) dollars per share.
2. A credit to the amount of the subscription price will be due in the amount of _____ ($_____) dollars, therein representing actual cash advances made by the undersigned or in behalf of the undersigned through the incorporation date of the aforesaid Corporation.
3. The full subscription price will be payable in cash, check or money order.
4. Payment of the full subscription price will be due on the _____ day of _____, 20__
5. The aforesaid Corporation, at the written request of undersigned, shall transfer as fully paid and non-assessable, any and all shares of stock that shall be fully paid by the undersigned. In addition, the proper Officer or Officers of the Corporation shall issue a new certificate or certificates for such shares transferred. In the event that less than all of the shares subscribed for by the undersigned are transferred, the proper Officer or Officers of the Corporation shall issue to the undersigned a new certificate or certificates, therein representing the difference between the number of shares as actually subscribed and the number of shares actually transferred.

In Witness Whereof, the parties have set their hands this _____ Day of _____ 20____.

_____   _____
Investor   Corporate Secretary
RESOLUTION OF THE BOARD OF DIRECTORS OF

AUTHORIZATION FOR ISSUANCE OF CORPORATE STOCK FOR SERVICES RENDERED BY OFFICER OR DIRECTOR

The Secretary announced that pursuant to the Articles of Incorporation and/or Bylaws of the above named Corporation, a special meeting of the Directors was held on the _____ day of _____, 20___ at _____ o'clock __M. The chairman then declared that the meeting was to be held in compliance with applicable statutes.

WHEREAS, _____, an Officer of the Board of Directors of the afore-said Corporation, has rendered valuable services to the Corporation, and said services have greatly benefited the Corporation, without charge to the Corporation, be it **RESOLVED**, that the Board of Directors of the aforesaid Corporation herewith grant the issuance of Corporation Stock to the above named person, in the amount of _____ (_____) shares of Stock, that said stock is fully paid and non-assessable in consideration for the full and total services rendered by said person, and said issuance of stock is a full and total release of the Corporation from any and all current and future liability for the services rendered, as mentioned supra.

CERTIFICATION OF CORPORATE SECRETARY

I the undersigned, certify that I am the duly appointed Secretary of the above named Corporation and that the forgoing Resolution is a true and accurate copy of a Resolution duly adopted at a meeting of the Shareholders thereof, convened and held in accordance with the Bylaws of said Corporation and that the Resolution is now in full force and effect.

IN WITNESS THEREOF, I have affixed my name as Secretary of the above named Corporation and have attached the seal of said Corporation to this Resolution.

Dated _____ 20___

_____
Corporate Secretary

RESOLUTION OF
(Replace This With The Name Of Your Corp)
A (Name of State) CORPORATION
FOR
AUTHORIZE SALE/LEASEBACK TRANSACTION

The Secretary announced that pursuant to the Articles of Incorporation and/or Bylaws of the above named Corporation, a special meeting of the Directors was held on the _____ day of _____, 20____ at _____ o'clock ___M. The chairman then declared that the meeting was to be held in compliance with applicable statutes.

WHEREAS, it is advisable for the Corporation to raise capital through a sale/leaseback of certain of its assets. Therefore, be it **RESOLVED** and **ORDERED**, that the Corporation sell and lease back the following property to the highest "bidder":

Description: _____

_____

_____

Sale price: $_____

And that concurrently the Corporation executes a lease for said property for a period of _____ years at a net annual rental not to exceed _____ (_____%) percent of the sales price, all in accord with generally prevailing sales/leaseback terms.

CERTIFICATION OF CORPORATE SECRETARY

I the undersigned, certify that I am the duly appointed Secretary of the above named Corporation and that the forgoing Resolution is a true and accurate copy of a Resolution duly adopted at a meeting of the Shareholders thereof, convened and held in accordance with the Bylaws of said Corporation and that the Resolution is now in full force and effect.

IN WITNESS THEREOF, I have affixed my name as Secretary of the above named Corporation and have attached the seal of said Corporation to this Resolution.

Dated _____ 20____

_____
Corporate Secretary

RESOLUTION OF THE BOARD OF DIRECTORS OF
(Replace This With The Name Of Your Corp)
A *(Name of State)* CORPORATION
TO
SELL CORPORATE PROPERTY

The Secretary announced that pursuant to the Articles of Incorporation and/or Bylaws of the above named Corporation, a special meeting of the Directors was held on the _____ day of _____, 20____ at _____ o'clock __M. The chairman then declared that the meeting was to be held in compliance with applicable statutes.

RESOLVED, that the Board of Directors of this Corporation is authorized to sell or exchange all or any part of this Corporation's property and assets, whether personal, tangible or intangible, including goodwill, upon such terms and conditions as the Board of Directors shall determine are in the best interests of the Corporation.

CERTIFICATION OF CORPORATE SECRETARY

I the undersigned, certify that I am the duly appointed Secretary of the above named Corporation and that the forgoing Resolution is a true and accurate copy of a Resolution duly adopted at a meeting of the Shareholders thereof, convened and held in accordance with the Bylaws of said Corporation and that the Resolution is now in full force and effect.

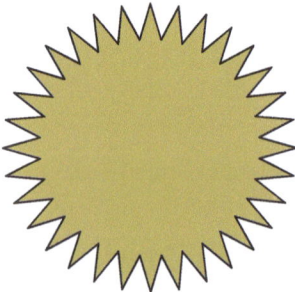

IN WITNESS THEREOF, I have affixed my name as Secretary of the above named Corporation and have attached the seal of said Corporation to this Resolution.

Dated _____ 20____

_____
Corporate Secretary

RESOLUTION OF THE BOARD OF DIRECTORS OF
(Replace This With The Name Of Your Corp)
A *(Name of State)* CORPORATION
TO
SELL REAL PROPERTY

The Secretary announced that pursuant to the Articles of Incorporation and/or Bylaws of the above named Corporation, a special meeting of the Directors was held on the _____ day of _____, 20___ at _____ o'clock __M. The chairman then declared that the meeting was to be held in compliance with applicable statutes.

WHEREAS, the Corporation is in need of additional capital, and

WHEREAS, the Corporation owns certain real estate that is no longer needed and that it would further be desirous to sell some; be it; **RESOLVED**, that the Corporation sell real estate known or described as _____ in the city of _____, county of _____, state of _____ for the most advantageous return to the Corporation, as further set forth in a sales agreement as annexed hereto.

Further, it is **RESOLVED** and **ORDERED**, that the Board of Directors of this Corporation be instructed to locate a suitable buyer for said sale and to execute all required documents for it.

CERTIFICATION OF CORPORATE SECRETARY

I the undersigned, certify that I am the duly appointed Secretary of the above named Corporation and that the forgoing Resolution is a true and accurate copy of a Resolution duly adopted at a meeting of the Shareholders thereof, convened and held in accordance with the Bylaws of said Corporation and that the Resolution is now in full force and effect.

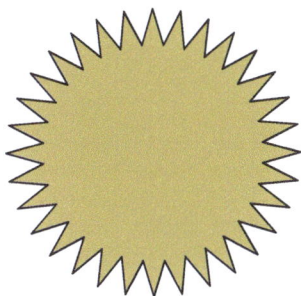

IN WITNESS THEREOF, I have affixed my name as Secretary of the above named Corporation and have attached the seal of said Corporation to this Resolution.

Dated _____ 20___

_____
Corporate Secretary

RESOLUTION OF
(Replace This With The Name Of Your Corp)
A (Name of State) CORPORATION
FOR
AUTHORIZED SIGNATORY FOR CORPORATION

The Secretary announced that pursuant to the Articles of Incorporation and/or Bylaws of the above named Corporation, a special meeting of the Directors was held on the _____ day of _____, 20___ at _____ o'clock __M. The chairman then declared that the meeting was to be held in compliance with applicable statutes.

The chairman of the meeting then discussed granting full signatory authority to _____ to sign any and all banking documents or instruments, contracts and/or any other documents as needed on behalf of this Corporation.

The chairman of the meeting then requested that the Board confer upon the above named individual full signatory authority to represent the interests of this Corporation in signing all banking documents or instruments negotiating and executing contract(s) and or any and all other documents relating to this Corporation.

On motion duly made and carried, it was, **RESOLVED** and **ORDERED** that the person named above, is henceforth granted the full signatory authority and power to enter into any and all agreements as necessary, and to negotiate and execute contract(s) or any other necessary documents relating to this Corporation.

CERTIFICATION OF CORPORATE SECRETARY

I the undersigned, certify that I am the duly appointed Secretary of the above named Corporation and that the forgoing Resolution is a true and accurate copy of a Resolution duly adopted at a meeting of the Shareholders thereof, convened and held in accordance with the Bylaws of said Corporation and that the Resolution is now in full force and effect.

IN WITNESS THEREOF, I have affixed my name as Secretary of the above named Corporation and have attached the seal of said Corporation to this Resolution.

Dated _____ 20___

_____
Corporate Secretary

MINUTES OF A SPECIAL MEETING
OF THE DIRECTORS OF
(Replace This With The Name Of Your Corp)
A *(Name of State)* CORPORATION
FOR
USE OF PERSONAL CREDIT

The Secretary announced that pursuant to the Articles of Incorporation and/or Bylaws of the above named Corporation, a special meeting of the Directors was held on the _____ day of _____, 20____ at _____ o'clock ___M. The chairman then declared that the meeting was to be held in compliance with applicable statutes.

The chairman of the meeting then discussed having one or more of the corporate officers/directors of the above named Corporation use their personal credit and/or credit cards to facilitate the needs of the Corporation due to the fact that the Corporation while earning money, has no credit history (credit worthiness) and the officers/directors in question have credit worthiness but lack financial resources.

On motion duly made and carried, it was **RESOLVED** and **ORDERED** that the following individuals would be authorized to state the Corporation's income on any application for credit (intended for the use of the Corporation only) in conjunction with said officers/directors personal credit history in order to secure credit and or credit cards to be primarily used for the benefit of this Corporation. In addition, it was **RESOLVED** and **ORDERED** that this Corporation shall directly pay (by check) all charges associated with the issuance of said credit/cards and/or the payment for any purchases using said credit/cards by this Corporation.

_____
Printed Name

_____
Signature

CERTIFICATION OF CORPORATE SECRETARY

I the undersigned, certify that I am the duly appointed Secretary of the above named Corporation and that the forgoing Resolution is a true and accurate copy of a Resolution duly adopted at a meeting of the Shareholders thereof, convened and held in accordance with the Bylaws of said Corporation and that the Resolution is now in full force and effect.

IN WITNESS THEREOF, I have affixed my name as Secretary of the above named Corporation and have attached the seal of said Corporation to this Resolution.

Dated _____ 20____

_____
Corporate Secretary

Asset Protection Services of America

**Limited Liability Company
Documents**

AssetProtectionServices.com

RESOLUTION OF MEMBERS OF
(Replace This With The Name Of Your LLC)
A *(Name of State)* LIMITED LIABILITY COMPANY
TO
ACQUIRE ASSETS OF A BUSINESS

The Secretary announced that pursuant to the Operating Agreement of the above named Limited Liability Company, a special meeting of the Members was held on the _____ day of _____, 20___ at _____ o'clock __M. The chairman then declared that the meeting was to be held in compliance with applicable statutes.

WHEREAS, it is in the best interests of the Company to acquire the assets of the following entity as a going concern _____*(put in the business name).*

It is hereby **RESOLVED**, that the Company execute an agreement to purchase the business assets of the above-stated entity as per the **Purchase Agreement** attached hereto; and

It is further **RESOLVED**, that the Managing Member or other Member of the Company named _____ be and is hereby authorized to execute such further documents and undertake such other acts as are reasonably required to carry out and conclude said transaction to purchase assets.

_____   _____
Member   Member

_____   _____
Member   Member

CERTIFICATION OF COMPANY SECRETARY

I the undersigned, certify that I am the duly appointed Secretary of the above named Company and that the forgoing Resolution is a true and accurate copy of a Resolution duly adopted at a meeting of the Members thereof, convened and held in accordance with the Operating Agreement of said Company and that the Resolution is now in full force and effect.

IN WITNESS THEREOF, I have affixed my name as Secretary of the above named Company and have attached the seal of said Company to this Resolution.

Dated _____ 20___

_____
Company Secretary

NOTICE OF MEETING OF MEMBERS OF
(Replace This With The Name Of Your LLC)
A *(Name of State)* LIMITED LIABILITY COMPANY
TO
ADD NEW MEMBERS

The Secretary announced that pursuant to the Operating Agreement of the above named Limited Liability Company, a special meeting of the Members was held on the _____ day of _____, 20____ at _____ o'clock ___M. The chairman then declared that the meeting was to be held in compliance with applicable statutes.

The purpose of the meeting is to consider increasing the number of Members of the Company and amending the operating agreement in connection therewith.

This Notice given on this the the _____ day of _____, 20____, by a _____ Member / _____ Manager of the Company, by mailing a true and correct copy of this Notice to the address of each Member of the Company at least 10 days prior to such meeting.

_____
Member / Manager

RESOLUTION OF MEMBERS OF
(Replace This With The Name Of Your LLC)
A *(Name of State)* LIMITED LIABILITY COMPANY
FOR
ADDING NEW MEMBERS

The Secretary announced that pursuant to the Operating Agreement of the above named Limited Liability Company, a special meeting of the Members was held on the _____ day of _____, 20____ at _____ o'clock ___M. The chairman then declared that the meeting was to be held in compliance with applicable statutes.

The purpose of the meeting was to consider increasing the number of Members of the Company and amending the operating agreement in connection therewith.

Upon motion duly made and seconded, the Members approved the following resolution and **RESOLVED** that the Members of the Company are increased from _____ (_____) to _____ (_____) and the following persons are admitted as Members subject to the condition below:

_____   _____
Member   Member

_____   _____
Member   Member

The Condition of their being admitted as Members is:

_____

_____

_____

SO RESOLVED, There being no further business, the meeting was adjourned.

_____
Managing Member

AMENDMENT TO
ARTICLES OF ORGANIZATION AND/OR OPERATING AGREEMENT
FOR
(Replace This With The Name Of Your LLC)
A *(Name of State)* LIMITED LIABILITY COMPANY

There was presented to the Members an amendment to the _____ Articles of Organization / _____ Operating Agreement for the Company. After consideration by the Members of the Company, it was **RESOLVED,** that the following amendment be made:

_____

_____

_____

_____

_____

The Secretary shall amend the document, file the document with the proper state agencies, if necessary, and distribute the amended document to the Members of the Company.

_____   _____
Member   Member

_____   _____
Member   Member

_____   _____
Member   Member

SO RESOLVED, There being no further business, the meeting was adjourned.

_____
Managing Member

NOTICE OF MEETING OF MEMBERS OF
(Replace This With The Name Of Your LLC)
A *(Name of State)* LIMITED LIABILITY COMPANY
FOR
ANNUAL DISBURSEMENTS TO MEMBERS

The Secretary announced that pursuant to the Operating Agreement of the above named Limited Liability Company, a special meeting of the Members was held on the _____ day of _____, 20____ at _____ o'clock ___M. The chairman then declared that the meeting was to be held in compliance with applicable statutes.

The purpose of the meeting is to consider annual disbursements to the Members of the Company. At the meeting the Company proposes to seek disbursement to the Members of the Company of _____ ($ _____) dollars in accordance with the Operating Agreement of the Company to the following Members:

_____   _____
Member   Member

_____   _____
Member   Member

_____   _____
Member   Member

This Notice given on this the _____ day of _____, 20____, by a _____ Manager / _____ Member of the Company, by mailing a true and correct copy of this Notice to the address of each Member of the Company at least 10 days prior to such meeting.

_____
Manager / Manager

RESOLUTION OF MEMBERS OF
(Replace This With The Name Of Your LLC)
A (Name of State) LIMITED LIABILITY COMPANY
FOR
ANNUAL DISBURSEMENTS TO MEMBERS

The Secretary announced that pursuant to the Operating Agreement of the above named Limited Liability Company, a special meeting of the Members was held on the _____ day of _____, 20___ at _____ o'clock ___M. The chairman then declared that the meeting was to be held in compliance with applicable statutes.

WHEREAS, it is in the best interests of the Company, the Members of the Company unanimously adopted the following resolution.

RESOLVED, annual disbursements to the Members of the Company shall be made as follows:

_____	$_____	_____	$_____
Member	Amount	Member	Amount
_____	$_____	_____	$_____
Member	Amount	Member	Amount
_____	$_____	_____	$_____
Member	Amount	Member	Amount

_____ $_____
Manager   Amount

SO RESOLVED, there being no further business, the meeting was adjourned.

_____   _____
Member   Member

_____   _____
Member   Member

_____   _____
Member   Member

_____
Managing Member

MINUTES OF THE ANNUAL MEETING OF MEMBERS
OF
(Replace This With The Name Of Your LLC)
A *(Name of State)* LIMITED LIABILITY COMPANY

The annual Meeting of Members of the above named Limited Liability Company was held on this _____ 20____ at 3:00 p.m. and at the place set forth in the written waiver of notice signed by all the Members, fixing such time and place, and prefixed to the minutes of this meeting. There were present at the meeting all of the Members of the above named Limited Liability Company.

_____

Member

_____

Member

_____

Member

_____

Member

_____

Member

_____

Member

The meeting was called to order by _____ it was moved, seconded and unanimously carried that _____ act as Chairman and that _____ act as Secretary.

The Chairman then stated that all of the Members were present. The Managing Member presented his/hers annual report and, after discussion, the report was accepted and ordered filed with the Secretary.

The Chairman noted that it was in order to consider electing managing members for the ensuing year. Upon nominations duly made and seconded, the following were unanimously elected Managing Members of the Limited Liability Company, to serve for the ensuing year and until their successors are elected and qualified:

     Managing Member: _____

     Managing Member: _____

     Secretary/ Treasurer: _____

CERTIFICATION OF COMPANY SECRETARY

I the undersigned, certify that I am the duly appointed Secretary of the above named Company and that the forgoing Resolution is a true and accurate copy of a Resolution duly adopted at a meeting of the Members thereof, convened and held in accordance with the Operating Agreement of said Company and that the Resolution is now in full force and effect.

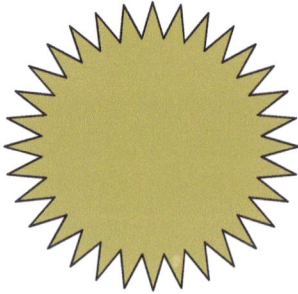

IN WITNESS THEREOF, I have affixed my name as Secretary of the above named Company and have attached the seal of said Company to this Resolution.

Dated _____ 20___

_____
Company Secretary

WAIVER OF NOTICE OF ANNUAL MEETING OF MEMBERS
OF
(Replace This With The Name Of Your LLC)
A *(Name of State)* LIMITED LIABILITY COMPANY

WE, the undersigned, being all of the Members of the Company, hereby agree and consent that the annual meeting of Members of the Company be held on the date and time and at the place designated hereunder, and do hereby waive all notice whatsoever of such meeting and of any adjournment or adjournments thereof.

We do agree and consent that any and all lawful business may be transacted at such meeting or at any adjournment or adjournments thereof as may be deemed advisable by the Members present threat. Any business transacted at such meeting or at any adjournment or adjournments thereof shall be as valid and legal and of the same force and effect as if such meeting or adjourned meeting were held after notice.

Place of Meeting: _____

Date of Meeting: _____

Time of Meeting: _____

Purpose of Meeting:_____

Manager: _____

Manager: _____

Member: _____

Member: _____

Member: _____

Member: _____

APPROVAL OF TRANSACTION BENEFITING MEMBERS
FOR
(Replace This With The Name Of Your LLC)
A *(Name of State)* LIMITED LIABILITY COMPANY

There was presented to the Members the following transaction:

_____

_____

_____

_____

_____

The transaction has a potential benefit to one or more Members of the Company. After consideration by the Members of the Company, it is hereby **RESOLVED,** that the above-described transaction has been approved.

_____   _____
Member   Member

_____   _____
Member   Member

_____   _____
Member   Member

ASSIGNMENT OF MEMBER INTEREST
IN
(Replace This With The Name Of Your LLC)
A *(Name of State)* LIMITED LIABILITY COMPANY

For Valuable Consideration, the receipt and sufficient of which, is herby acknowledged, I the undersigned "Assignor", Member of the above named Limited Liability Company, hereinafter "Company", does hereby assign, transfer and warrant to _____, "Assignee", all of Members ownership interest in the Company.

Except as otherwise provided in the operating agreement, a Membership interest in a Limited Liability Company is assignable in whole or in part. The Operating Agreement of the Company does not prohibit assignment of a Member interest. An Assignment of this interest does not dissolve the Company or entitle the Assignee to become or to exercise any rights of a Member. An assignment entitles the Assignee to receive, to the extent assigned, the distributions of cash and other property and the allocations of profits, losses, income, gains, deductions, credits, or similar items to which the Assignee's Assignor would have been entitled. The Assignor ceases to be a Member upon assignment of all the Assignor's membership interest. Except as provided herein, until Assignee becomes a Member, the Assignee does not have liability as a Member solely because of the assignment.

Assignee may become a Member if and to the extent that the Assignor gives the Assignee that right and either of the following occurs:

1. The Assignor has been given the authority in writing in the Operating Agreement to give an Assignee the right to become a Member.

2. All other Members consent.

By execution hereof, Assignor, gives to Assignee the right to become a Member of the Company. Once Assignee becomes a Member, he has to the extent assigned the rights and powers of a Member under the Operating Agreement are subject to the restrictions and liabilities of a Member under the Operating Agreement. Assignee is liable for the obligations of Assignor to make contributions as provided by law. Assignee is not obligated for liabilities hat could not be ascertained from a written Operating Agreement and that were unknown to Assignee at the time he becomes a Member.

Assignor is not released from his liability to a Limited Liability Company for the past capital contributions required by law whether or not the Assignee becomes a Member.

Dated This _____, 20____

_____
Member

RESOLUTION OF THE MEMBERS OF
(Replace This With The Name Of Your LLC)
A *(Name of State)* LIMITED LIABILITY COMPANY
FOR
BILL OF SALE & AGREEMENT

The Secretary announced that pursuant to the Operating Agreement of the above named Limited Liability Company, a special meeting of the Members was held on the _____ day of _____, 20____ at _____ o'clock ___M. The chairman then declared that the meeting was to be held in compliance with applicable statutes.

The purpose of the meeting was to consider the purchase all rights, title and interest in the property and assets shown on **ATTACHMENT "A"** that must be attached hereto and thereby made a part hereof.

In return for the transfer of said property, the Company agrees to assume, pay and discharge all debts, duties and obligations that exist as of the date of transfer to this Company. Further, the Company agrees to indemnify and hold transferor free from any liability for any such debts, duties and obligations, suits, actions, or legal proceedings brought to enforce or collect such debt, duty or obligation.

In addition, appoints the Company to do all things allowed by law to demand, receive, and collect for itself any debt or obligation now owing and authorizes it to recover and collect any such debt or obligation and to use the name(s) of transferor in such manner as it considers necessary to collect and recover such debts or obligations

CERTIFICATION OF COMPANY SECRETARY

I the undersigned, certify that I am the duly appointed Secretary of the above named Company and that the forgoing Resolution is a true and accurate copy of a Resolution duly adopted at a meeting of the Members thereof, convened and held in accordance with the Operating Agreement of said Company and that the Resolution is now in full force and effect.

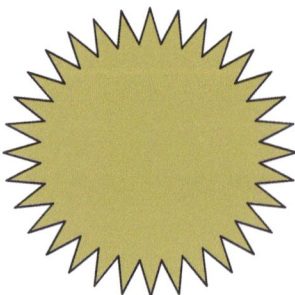

IN WITNESS THEREOF, I have affixed my name as Secretary of the above named Company and have attached the seal of said Company to this Resolution.

Dated _____ 20____

_____
Company Secretary

BLANK MEMBER'S RESOLUTION
OF
(Replace This With The Name Of Your LLC)
A *(Name of State)* LIMITED LIABILITY COMPANY
TO

_____

The Secretary announced that pursuant to the Operating Agreement of the above named Limited Liability Company, a special meeting of the Members was held on the _____ day of _____, 20___ at _____ o'clock __M. The chairman then declared that the meeting was to be held in compliance with applicable statutes.

The chairman of the meeting then discussed:

_____

_____

_____

On motion duly made and carried, it was **RESOLVED** and **ORDERED** that:

_____

_____

_____

CERTIFICATION OF COMPANY SECRETARY

I the undersigned, certify that I am the duly appointed Secretary of the above named Company and that the forgoing Resolution is a true and accurate copy of a Resolution duly adopted at a meeting of the Members thereof, convened and held in accordance with the Operating Agreement of said Company and that the Resolution is now in full force and effect.

IN WITNESS THEREOF, I have affixed my name as Secretary of the above named Company and have attached the seal of said Company to this Resolution.

Dated _____ 20___

_____

Company Secretary

RESOLUTION OF THE MEMBERS OF
(Replace This With The Name Of Your LLC)
A (Name of State) LIMITED LIABILITY COMPANY
TO
BORROW CAPITAL

The Secretary announced that pursuant to the Operating Agreement of the above named Limited Liability Company, a special meeting of the Members was held on the _____ day of _____, 20___ at _____ o'clock __M. The chairman then declared that the meeting was to be held in compliance with applicable statutes.

WHEREAS, the Company is in need of additional capital, and

WHEREAS, _____, _____ as a Member of the Company, has agreed to loan to the Company the sum of _____ ($ _____), and

WHEREAS, such borrowing appears to be advantageous to the Company as it is on better terms than would be available elsewhere; be it: **RESOLVED** and **ORDERED**, that the Company borrow the sum of _____ ($ _____), from the above named Member and that said sum be repaid in or within _____ (____) years with interest thereon at _____ (_____%) on the unpaid balance, all as more fully set forth in a promissory note and collateral loan documents that when executed, must be placed in the minutes of this Company.

CERTIFICATION OF COMPANY SECRETARY

I the undersigned, certify that I am the duly appointed Secretary of the above named Company and that the forgoing Resolution is a true and accurate copy of a Resolution duly adopted at a meeting of the Members thereof, convened and held in accordance with the Operating Agreement of said Company and that the Resolution is now in full force and effect.

IN WITNESS THEREOF, I have affixed my name as Secretary of the above named Company and have attached the seal of said Company to this Resolution.

Dated _____ 20___

_____
Company Secretary

RESOLUTION OF THE MEMBERS OF
(Replace This With The Name Of Your LLC)
A *(Name of State)* LIMITED LIABILITY COMPANY
TO
BORROW ON ACCOUNTS RECEIVABLE, EQUIPMENT, INVENTORY

The Secretary announced that pursuant to the Operating Agreement of the above named Limited Liability Company, a special meeting of the Members was held on the _____ day of _____, 20___ at _____ o'clock __M. The chairman then declared that the meeting was to be held in compliance with applicable statutes.

RESOLVED and **ORDERED**, that the President of this Company, is hereby authorized and directed to borrow the sum of _____ ($ _____), from any entity or individual on the terms set out in a contract or Promissory Note which when executed must be placed in the minutes of this meeting and to execute a mortgage in favor of the Lender covering the accounts receivable, equipment, fixtures, furniture, inventory or merchandise set out in a Schedule attached to the minutes of this meeting.

Therefore, it is **FURTHER RESOLVED** and **ORDERED**, that the Member of the Company is hereby authorized and directed to provide for creditors of the Company all notices required by law to be given to the creditors of the Company, and to do everything else that may be necessary to complete the authorized transaction.

CERTIFICATION OF COMPANY SECRETARY

I the undersigned, certify that I am the duly appointed Secretary of the above named Company and that the forgoing Resolution is a true and accurate copy of a Resolution duly adopted at a meeting of the Members thereof, convened and held in accordance with the Operating Agreement of said Company and that the Resolution is now in full force and effect.

IN WITNESS THEREOF, I have affixed my name as Secretary of the above named Company and have attached the seal of said Company to this Resolution.

Dated _____ 20___

_____
Company Secretary

CAPITAL CONTRIBUTION OF MEMBERS
OF
(Replace This With The Name Of Your LLC)
A *(Name of State)* LIMITED LIABILITY COMPANY
AS OF _____, 20___

*(**NOTE:** Capital contributions can be cash or the value of providing services, property, equipment, supplies, etc.)*

(1) Member's Name: _____

Complete Address: _____

_____

Capital Contribution: $_____

Percentage Interest: _____ (_____%)

(2) Member's Name: _____

Complete Address: _____

_____

Capital Contribution: $_____

Percentage Interest: _____ (_____%)

(3) Member's Name: _____

Complete Address: _____

_____

Capital Contribution: $_____

Percentage Interest: _____ (_____%)

(4) Member's Name: _____

Complete Address: _____

_____

Capital Contribution: $_____

Percentage Interest: _____ (_____%)

(5) Member's Name: _____

Complete Address: _____

_____

Capital Contribution: $_____

Percentage Interest: _____ (_____%)

(6) Member's Name: _____

Complete Address: _____

_____

Capital Contribution: $_____

Percentage Interest: _____ (_____%)

(7) Member's Name: _____

Complete Address: _____

_____

Capital Contribution: $_____

Percentage Interest: _____ (_____%)

The Secretary announced that pursuant to the Operating Agreement of the above named Limited Liability Company, a special meeting of the Members was held on the _____ day of _____, 20____ at _____ o'clock ___M. The chairman then declared that the meeting was to be held in compliance with applicable statutes.

By signing this document, the undersigned, which are all of the _____ Managers / _____ Members of the above named Company, consent to the taking of the following actions without a meeting of the managers or members in accordance with the terms of the Operating Agreement of the Company:

RESOLVED, that _____ is elected to serve as a Manager of the Company for a term beginning on the date of this consent to action and ending at the next meeting of Members of the Company called for the purpose of electing Managers, or the Manager's death, resignation, or removal, if earlier.

RESOLVED, that

_____

_____

_____

is authorized and the above named Managing Member is hereby directed to do all things necessary to complete the transaction herein above discussed.

The actions taken will be effective when this Consent to Action has been singed by all _____ Managers / _____ Members of the Company.

_____   _____
Member   Member

_____   _____
Member   Member

_____   _____
Managing Member   Managing Member

MINUTES OF A SPECIAL MEETING OF
(Replace This With The Name Of Your LLC)
A (Name of State) LIMITED LIABILITY COMPANY
FOR
DEMISE OR INCAPACITATION OF MEMBERS

The Secretary announced that pursuant to the Operating Agreement of the above named Limited Liability Company, a special meeting of the Members was held on the _____ day of _____, 20___ at _____ o'clock ___M. The chairman then declared that the meeting was to be held in compliance with applicable statutes.

The chairman of the meeting then discussed electing assistant Member who shall immediately replace their respective elected Members in case of the demise or incapacitation of any or all of the current Members of this Company pursuant to the Operating Agreement of this Company. On motion duly made and carried, it was; **RESOLVED** and **ORDERED** that the following individual be elected and has accepted the respective office at the meeting:

ASSISTANT MANAGER: _____

The chairman of the meeting then discussed electing substitute signatories on any and all Company bank accounts and merchant accounts for this Company in case of the demise or incapacitation of any or all of the current signatories of this Company. On motion duly made and carried, it was; **RESOLVED** and **ORDERED** that the following individual be elected as substitute signatories on any and all Company bank accounts and merchant accounts for this Company in case of the demise or incapacitation of any or all of the current signatories of this Company and each has accepted their respective offices at the meeting:

_____   _____
Printed Name   Signature

CERTIFICATION OF COMPANY SECRETARY

I the undersigned, certify that I am the duly appointed Secretary of the above named Company and that the forgoing Resolution is a true and accurate copy of a Resolution duly adopted at a meeting of the Members thereof, convened and held in accordance with the Operating Agreement of said Company and that the Resolution is now in full force and effect.

IN WITNESS THEREOF, I have affixed my name as Secretary of the above named Company and have attached the seal of said Company to this Resolution.

Dated _____ 20___

_____
Company Secretary

RESOLUTION OF
(Replace This With The Name Of Your LLC)
A *(Name of State)* LIMITED LIABILITY COMPANY
FOR
DISSOLUTION OF LIMITED LIABILITY COMPANY

The Secretary announced that pursuant to the Operating Agreement of the above named Limited Liability Company, a special meeting of the Members was held on the _____ day of _____, 20____ at _____ o'clock ___M. The chairman then declared that the meeting was to be held in compliance with applicable statutes.

RESOLVED that _____ shall dissolve forthwith, and it is:

FURTHER RESOLVED and **ORDERED**, that the Managing Member of the Company is hereby authorized and directed to file the necessary Certificate of Dissolution of this Limited Liability Company with Secretary of State in accordance with the laws of the State of

_____.

CERTIFICATION OF COMPANY SECRETARY

I the undersigned, certify that I am the duly appointed Secretary of the above named Company and that the forgoing Resolution is a true and accurate copy of a Resolution duly adopted at a meeting of the Members thereof, convened and held in accordance with the Operating Agreement of said Company and that the Resolution is now in full force and effect.

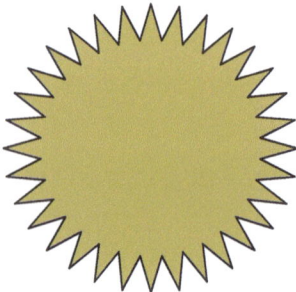

IN WITNESS THEREOF, I have affixed my name as Secretary of the above named Company and have attached the seal of said Company to this Resolution.

Dated _____ 20____

_____
Company Secretary

RESOLUTION OF THE MEMBERS OF
(Replace This With The Name Of Your LLC)
A *(Name of State)* LIMITED LIABILITY COMPANY
TO
LOAN FUNDS TO MEMBER

The Secretary announced that pursuant to the Operating Agreement of the above named Limited Liability Company, a special meeting of the Members was held on the _____ day of _____, 20____ at _____ o'clock ___M. The chairman then declared that the meeting was to be held in compliance with applicable statutes.

WHEREAS, _____ a Member of this Company, has requested of this Company an advance and/or loan in the amount of _____ ($ _____), together with interest, and

WHEREAS, the Company has adequate financial resources to make such loan without impairing its growth or profitability, and that said loan is deemed reasonably secure and in the best interests of the Company to make, be it **RESOLVED** and **ORDERED**, that the Company issue a loan to _____ in the amount of _____ ($ _____), to be repaid within _____ (____) months with interest of _____ (_____%) on the unpaid balance, and that the borrower execute to the Company a promissory note evidencing said indebtedness.

CERTIFICATION OF COMPANY SECRETARY

I the undersigned, certify that I am the duly appointed Secretary of the above named Company and that the forgoing Resolution is a true and accurate copy of a Resolution duly adopted at a meeting of the Members thereof, convened and held in accordance with the Operating Agreement of said Company and that the Resolution is now in full force and effect.

IN WITNESS THEREOF, I have affixed my name as Secretary of the above named Company and have attached the seal of said Company to this Resolution.

Dated _____ 20____

_____
Company Secretary

MEETING PARTICIPANT LIST
FOR
(Replace This With The Name Of Your LLC)
A *(Name of State)* LIMITED LIABILITY COMPANY

Type of Meeting: _____ Regular; or
_____ Special

Meeting of: _____ Managers; and/or
_____ Members

Date: _____ 20____ Time: 3:00 p.m.

Meetings Participants: Manager: _____

Manager: _____

Member: _____

Member: _____

Member: _____

Member: _____

RESOLUTION OF THE MEMBERS OF
(Replace This With The Name Of Your LLC)
A *(Name of State)* LIMITED LIABILITY COMPANY
TO
PURCHASE EQUIPMENT

The Secretary announced that pursuant to the Operating Agreement of the above named Limited Liability Company, a special meeting of the Members was held on the _____ day of _____, 20___ at _____ o'clock ___M. The chairman then declared that the meeting was to be held in compliance with applicable statutes.

WHEREAS, certain equipment is necessary for the operation of the business, therefore be it **RESOLVED** and **ORDERED**, that this Company shall purchase the following equipment:

Description: _____

Model Number: _____

Purchase From: _____

Purchase Price: $_____

To be paid: _____ Day _____ Week _____ Month

_____ Other _____

CERTIFICATION OF COMPANY SECRETARY

I the undersigned, certify that I am the duly appointed Secretary of the above named Company and that the forgoing Resolution is a true and accurate copy of a Resolution duly adopted at a meeting of the Members thereof, convened and held in accordance with the Operating Agreement of said Company and that the Resolution is now in full force and effect.

IN WITNESS THEREOF, I have affixed my name as Secretary of the above named Company and have attached the seal of said Company to this Resolution.

Dated _____ 20___

_____
Company Secretary

RESOLUTION OF THE MEMBERS OF
(Replace This With The Name Of Your LLC)
A *(Name of State)* LIMITED LIABILITY COMPANY
TO
PURCHASE MOTOR VEHICLES

The Secretary announced that pursuant to the Operating Agreement of the above named Limited Liability Company, a special meeting of the Members was held on the _____ day of _____, 20___ at _____ o'clock __M. The chairman then declared that the meeting was to be held in compliance with applicable statutes.

WHEREAS, motor vehicles are necessary for the operation of the business, therefore be it **RESOLVED** and **ORDERED**, that this Company shall purchase the motor vehicle(s) described as:

Description: _____

Model Number: _____

Lease/Rent From: _____

Lease/Rental price: $_____

To be paid: _____ Day _____ Week _____ Month

_____ Other _____

CERTIFICATION OF COMPANY SECRETARY

I the undersigned, certify that I am the duly appointed Secretary of the above named Company and that the forgoing Resolution is a true and accurate copy of a Resolution duly adopted at a meeting of the Members thereof, convened and held in accordance with the Operating Agreement of said Company and that the Resolution is now in full force and effect.

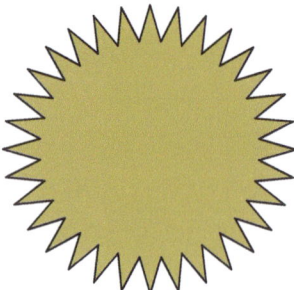

IN WITNESS THEREOF, I have affixed my name as Secretary of the above named Company and have attached the seal of said Company to this Resolution.

Dated _____ 20___

_____
Company Secretary

RESOLUTION OF THE MEMBERS OF
(Replace This With The Name Of Your LLC)
A *(Name of State)* LIMITED LIABILITY COMPANY
FOR
PURCHASE REAL PROPERTY

The Secretary announced that pursuant to the Operating Agreement of the above named Limited Liability Company, a special meeting of the Members was held on the _____ day of _____, 20____ at _____ o'clock ___M. The chairman then declared that the meeting was to be held in compliance with applicable statutes.

WHEREAS, the Company has decided to purchase various parcels of real estate under the terms of the attached **Real Estate Purchase Services Agreement**.

Therefore, be it: **RESOLVED** and **ORDERED**, that the Company purchase and acquire said real estate as set forth in the Real Estate Purchase Services Agreement as annexed hereto and that the named Authorized Signatory be authorized to represent this company as the signatory for any and all documentary requirements pertaining thereto.

There being no further business requiring Member action or consideration, and on a motion duly made, seconded and carried, the meeting was adjourned.

CERTIFICATION OF COMPANY SECRETARY

I the undersigned, certify that I am the duly appointed Secretary of the above named Company and that the forgoing Resolution is a true and accurate copy of a Resolution duly adopted at a meeting of the Members thereof, convened and held in accordance with the Operating Agreement of said Company and that the Resolution is now in full force and effect.

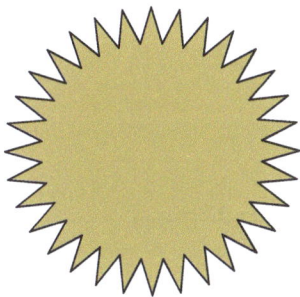

IN WITNESS THEREOF, I have affixed my name as Secretary of the above named Company and have attached the seal of said Company to this Resolution.

Dated _____ 20____

_____
Company Secretary

RESOLUTION OF
(Replace This With The Name Of Your LLC)
A *(Name of State)* LIMITED LIABILITY COMPANY
FOR
ESTABLISHING THE AUTHORIZED SIGNATORY FOR THE PURCHASE AND/OR SALE OF REAL PROPERTY

The Secretary announced that pursuant to the Operating Agreement of the above named Limited Liability Company, a special meeting of the Members was held on the _____ day of _____, 20___ at _____ o'clock __M. The chairman then declared that the meeting was to be held in compliance with applicable statutes.

The chairman of the meeting then discussed granting full signatory authority to the named Authorized Signatory to sign any and all banking documents or instruments, contracts and/or any other documents as needed on behalf of this Company. On motion duly made and carried, it was, **RESOLVED** and **ORDERED** that the named Authorized Signatory be henceforth granted the full signatory authority and power to grant, bargain, convey, sell, acquire or purchase; to sign promissory notes, mortgages or deeds of trust encumbering the property of this Company; to contract for the sale, conveyance, acquisition or purchase of any and all property belonging to this Company; to execute escrow instructions, trust agreements, agreements for sale, deeds or other conveyances of land, bills of sale, construction contracts, leases, subordinate agreements subordinating any lien, encumbrance or other right in real or personal property to any other lien or encumbrance or other contracts and/or instrument(s) necessary to effect such sale, conveyance, exchange, acquisition or purchase and to give warrantees to the purchasers thereof; to execute any and all documents deemed necessary without the attestation of the Members or affixing of the Company seal thereto and upon execution of such instruments by the named Authorized Signatory, such documents so executed shall be valid and binding without further act or specific resolution of the Members.

CERTIFICATION OF COMPANY SECRETARY

I the undersigned, certify that I am the duly appointed Secretary of the above named Company and that the forgoing Resolution is a true and accurate copy of a Resolution duly adopted at a meeting of the Members thereof, convened and held in accordance with the Operating Agreement of said Company and that the Resolution is now in full force and effect.

IN WITNESS THEREOF, I have affixed my name as Secretary of the above named Company and have attached the seal of said Company to this Resolution.

Dated _____ 20___

_____
Company Secretary

RESOLUTION OF THE MEMBERS OF
(Replace This With The Name Of Your LLC)
A *(Name of State)* LIMITED LIABILITY COMPANY
FOR
RENT/LEASE EQUIPMENT

The Secretary announced that pursuant to the Operating Agreement of the above named Limited Liability Company, a special meeting of the Members was held on the _____ day of _____, 20___ at _____ o'clock __M. The chairman then declared that the meeting was to be held in compliance with applicable statutes.

WHEREAS, certain equipment is necessary for the operation of the business, therefore be it **RESOLVED** and **ORDERED**, that this Company shall rent or lease the following equipment:

Year, Make and Model: _____

License Number _____

V.I.N. _____

Lease/Rent From: _____

Lease/Rental price: $_____

To be paid in: _____ CASH _____ CREDIT _____ OTHER:_____

CERTIFICATION OF COMPANY SECRETARY

I the undersigned, certify that I am the duly appointed Secretary of the above named Company and that the forgoing Resolution is a true and accurate copy of a Resolution duly adopted at a meeting of the Members thereof, convened and held in accordance with the Operating Agreement of said Company and that the Resolution is now in full force and effect.

IN WITNESS THEREOF, I have affixed my name as Secretary of the above named Company and have attached the seal of said Company to this Resolution.

Dated _____ 20___

_____
Company Secretary

RESOLUTION OF
(Replace This With The Name Of Your LLC)
A *(Name of State)* LIMITED LIABILITY COMPANY
TO
RENT/LEASE HOME OR OFFICE

The Secretary announced that pursuant to the Operating Agreement of the above named Limited Liability Company, a special meeting of the Members was held on the _____ day of _____, 20___ at _____ o'clock __M. The chairman then declared that the meeting was to be held in compliance with applicable statutes.

WHEREAS, it is necessary for the operation of the business of this Company to have an office location with living quarters in order for a Member of this Company to protect the property of this Company and to be able to undertake the business of the above named Company regardless of the hour day or night. Therefore be it **RESOLVED** and **ORDERED** that this Company shall rent or lease the following location pursuant to the attached lease agreement (in the Company name).

Office Location (Description): _____

Address: _____

Leased/Rented From (Land Lord): _____

Address: _____

There being no further business requiring Member action or consideration, and on a motion duly made, seconded and carried, the meeting was adjourned.

CERTIFICATION OF COMPANY SECRETARY

I the undersigned, certify that I am the duly appointed Secretary of the above named Company and that the forgoing Resolution is a true and accurate copy of a Resolution duly adopted at a meeting of the Members thereof, convened and held in accordance with the Operating Agreement of said Company and that the Resolution is now in full force and effect.

IN WITNESS THEREOF, I have affixed my name as Secretary of the above named Company and have attached the seal of said Company to this Resolution.

Dated _____ 20___

_____
Company Secretary

RESOLUTION OF
(Replace This With The Name Of Your LLC)
A *(Name of State)* LIMITED LIABILITY COMPANY
TO
RENT/LEASE MOTOR VEHICLES

The Secretary announced that pursuant to the Operating Agreement of the above named Limited Liability Company, a special meeting of the Members was held on the _____ day of _____, 20___ at _____ o'clock __M. The chairman then declared that the meeting was to be held in compliance with applicable statutes.

WHEREAS, certain vehicles are necessary for the operation of the business, therefore be it **RESOLVED** and **ORDERED**, that this Company shall rent or lease the following vehicles:

Year, Make and Model: _____

License Number: _____

V.I.N. _____

Purchase From: _____

Purchase price of: $_____

To be paid in: _____ Cash _____ Credit _____ Other:_____

CERTIFICATION OF COMPANY SECRETARY

I the undersigned, certify that I am the duly appointed Secretary of the above named Company and that the forgoing Resolution is a true and accurate copy of a Resolution duly adopted at a meeting of the Members thereof, convened and held in accordance with the Operating Agreement of said Company and that the Resolution is now in full force and effect.

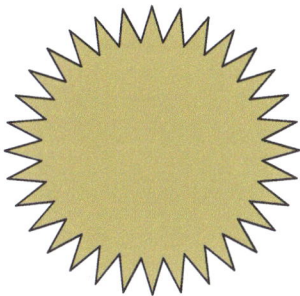

IN WITNESS THEREOF, I have affixed my name as Secretary of the above named Company and have attached the seal of said Company to this Resolution.

Dated _____ 20___

_____
Company Secretary

NOTICE OF MEETING OF MEMBERS OF
(Replace This With The Name Of Your LLC)
A *(Name of State)* LIMITED LIABILITY COMPANY
FOR
RESIGNATION AND REPLACEMENT OF
MANAGER OF COMPANY

The Secretary announced that pursuant to the Operating Agreement of the above named Limited Liability Company, a special meeting of the Members was held on the _____ day of _____, 20___ at _____ o'clock __M. The chairman then declared that the meeting was to be held in compliance with applicable statutes.

The purpose of acceptance of the resignation of the Manager of Company is to appoint a new Manager. Further to the resignation of _____ as the Manager of Company is hereby accepted and the appointment of _____ as the new Manager of Company has been approved and accepted by _____ on the date first written above.

This Notice given on this the _____ day of _____, 20___, by a _____ Member /_____ Manager of the Company, by mailing a true and correct copy of this Notice to the address of each Member of the Company.

_____
Member / Manager

CERTIFICATION OF COMPANY SECRETARY

I the undersigned, certify that I am the duly appointed Secretary of the above named Company and that the forgoing Resolution is a true and accurate copy of a Resolution duly adopted at a meeting of the Members thereof, convened and held in accordance with the Operating Agreement of said Company and that the Resolution is now in full force and effect.

IN WITNESS THEREOF, I have affixed my name as Secretary of the above named Company and have attached the seal of said Company to this Resolution.

Dated _____ 20___

_____
Company Secretary

RESOLUTION OF MEMBERS OF
(Replace This With The Name Of Your LLC)
A *(Name of State)* LIMITED LIABILITY COMPANY
FOR
SETTING MANAGING MEMBER SALARY

The Secretary announced that pursuant to the Operating Agreement of the above named Limited Liability Company, a special meeting of the Members was held on the _____ day of _____, 20___ at _____ o'clock __M. The chairman then declared that the meeting was to be held in compliance with applicable statutes.

WHEREAS, the Company desires to fill the position of Managing Member for the yearly gross salary of _____ ($_____) with all usual deductions and benefits;

It is hereby **RESOLVED**, that _____ be entered on the payroll records of the Company with salary stated above.

The salary of any Managing Member shall not commence until such time as the Company is profitable so as not to place the Company into financial distress by paying such salary.

_____   _____
Member   Member

_____   _____
Member   Member

_____   _____
Member   Member

CERTIFICATION OF COMPANY SECRETARY

I the undersigned, certify that I am the duly appointed Secretary of the above named Company and that the forgoing Resolution is a true and accurate copy of a Resolution duly adopted at a meeting of the Members thereof, convened and held in accordance with the Operating Agreement of said Company and that the Resolution is now in full force and effect.

IN WITNESS THEREOF, I have affixed my name as Secretary of the above named Company and have attached the seal of said Company to this Resolution.

Dated _____ 20___

_____
Company Secretary

RESOLUTION OF THE MEMBERS OF
(Replace This With The Name Of Your LLC)
A (Name of State) LIMITED LIABILITY COMPANY
FOR
AUTHORIZE SALE/LEASEBACK TRANSACTION

The Secretary announced that pursuant to the Operating Agreement of the above named Limited Liability Company, a special meeting of the Members was held on the _____ day of _____, 20___ at _____ o'clock __M. The chairman then declared that the meeting was to be held in compliance with applicable statutes.

The purpose of the meeting was to consider the advisability for the Company to raise capital through a sale/leaseback of certain of its assets. Therefore, be it **RESOLVED** and **ORDERED**, that the Company sell and lease back the following property to the highest "bidder":

Description: _____

_____

_____

Sale price: $_____

And that concurrently the Company execute a lease for said property for a period of _____ (___) years at a net annual rental not to exceed _____ (____%), percent of the sales price, all in accord with generally prevailing sales/leaseback terms.

CERTIFICATION OF COMPANY SECRETARY

I the undersigned, certify that I am the duly appointed Secretary of the above named Company and that the forgoing Resolution is a true and accurate copy of a Resolution duly adopted at a meeting of the Members thereof, convened and held in accordance with the Operating Agreement of said Company and that the Resolution is now in full force and effect.

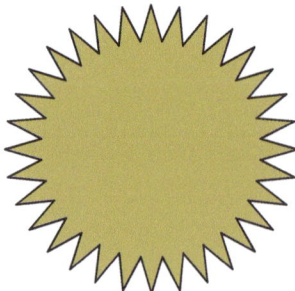

IN WITNESS THEREOF, I have affixed my name as Secretary of the above named Company and have attached the seal of said Company to this Resolution.

Dated _____ 20___

_____
Company Secretary

RESOLUTION OF THE MEMBERS OF
(Replace This With The Name Of Your LLC)
A (Name of State) LIMITED LIABILITY COMPANY
TO
SELL COMPANY PROPERTY

The Secretary announced that pursuant to the Operating Agreement of the above named Limited Liability Company, a special meeting of the Members was held on the _____ day of _____, 20___ at _____ o'clock __M. The chairman then declared that the meeting was to be held in compliance with applicable statutes.

RESOLVED, that the Managing Members of this Corporation are authorized to sell or exchange all or any part of this Company's property and assets, whether personal, tangible or intangible, including goodwill, upon such terms and conditions as the Managing Members shall determine are in the best interests of the Company.

CERTIFICATION OF COMPANY SECRETARY

I the undersigned, certify that I am the duly appointed Secretary of the above named Company and that the forgoing Resolution is a true and accurate copy of a Resolution duly adopted at a meeting of the Members thereof, convened and held in accordance with the Operating Agreement of said Company and that the Resolution is now in full force and effect.

IN WITNESS THEREOF, I have affixed my name as Secretary of the above named Company and have attached the seal of said Company to this Resolution.

Dated _____ 20___

_____
Company Secretary

RESOLUTION OF THE MEMBERS OF
(Replace This With The Name Of Your LLC)
A *(Name of State)* LIMITED LIABILITY COMPANY
TO
SELL REAL PROPERTY

The Secretary announced that pursuant to the Operating Agreement of the above named Limited Liability Company, a special meeting of the Members was held on the _____ day of _____, 20___ at _____ o'clock __M. The chairman then declared that the meeting was to be held in compliance with applicable statutes.

WHEREAS, the Company is in need of additional capital, and

WHEREAS, the Company owns certain real estate that is no longer needed and that it would further be desirous to sell some; be it; **RESOLVED**, that the Company sell real estate known or described as _____ in the city of _____, county of _____, state of _____ for the most advantageous return to the Company, as further set forth in a sales agreement as annexed hereto.

Further, it is **RESOLVED** and **ORDERED**, that the Managing Member of this Company be instructed to locate a suitable buyer for said sale and to execute all required documents for it.

CERTIFICATION OF COMPANY SECRETARY

I the undersigned, certify that I am the duly appointed Secretary of the above named Company and that the forgoing Resolution is a true and accurate copy of a Resolution duly adopted at a meeting of the Members thereof, convened and held in accordance with the Operating Agreement of said Company and that the Resolution is now in full force and effect.

IN WITNESS THEREOF, I have affixed my name as Secretary of the above named Company and have attached the seal of said Company to this Resolution.

Dated _____ 20___

_____
Company Secretary

RESOLUTION OF THE MEMBERS OF
(Replace This With The Name Of Your LLC)
A *(Name of State)* LIMITED LIABILITY COMPANY
FOR
AUTHORIZED SIGNATORY FOR COMPANY

The Secretary announced that pursuant to the Operating Agreement of the above named Limited Liability Company, a special meeting of the Members was held on the _____ day of _____, 20____ at _____ o'clock ___M. The chairman then declared that the meeting was to be held in compliance with applicable statutes.

The chairman of the meeting then discussed granting full signatory authority to _____ sign any and all banking documents or instruments, contracts and/or any other documents as needed on behalf of this Company.

The chairman of the meeting then requested that the Members confer upon the above named individual full signatory authority to represent the interests of this Company in signing all banking documents or instruments negotiating and executing contract(s) and or any and all other documents relating to this Company.

On motion duly made and carried, it was, **RESOLVED** and **ORDERED** that the person named above, is henceforth granted the full signatory authority and power to enter into any and all agreements as necessary, and to negotiate and execute contract(s) or any other necessary documents relating to this Company.

There being no further business requiring Member action or consideration on a motion duly made, seconded and carried, the meeting was adjourned.

CERTIFICATION OF COMPANY SECRETARY

I the undersigned, certify that I am the duly appointed Secretary of the above named Company and that the forgoing Resolution is a true and accurate copy of a Resolution duly adopted at a meeting of the Members thereof, convened and held in accordance with the Operating Agreement of said Company and that the Resolution is now in full force and effect.

IN WITNESS THEREOF, I have affixed my name as Secretary of the above named Company and have attached the seal of said Company to this Resolution.

Dated _____ 20____

_____
Company Secretary

MINUTES OF A SPECIAL MEETING OF MEMBERS OF
(Replace This With The Name Of Your LLC)
A *(Name of State)* LIMITED LIABILITY COMPANY
FOR
TERMINATION AND REPLACEMENT
OF MANAGING MEMBER

The Secretary announced that pursuant to the Operating Agreement of the above named Limited Liability Company, a special meeting of the Members was held on the _____ day of _____, 20___ at _____ o'clock __M. The chairman then declared that the meeting was to be held in compliance with applicable statutes.

The chairman of the meeting declared that the meeting was for the purpose of terminating the current Managing Member and to appoint a new Managing Member for the above named Company.

After a brief discussion and the unanimous agreement of the members, the chairman of the meeting stated that it was **RESOLVED** by unanimous agreement, that the termination of _____ as the Managing Member and the appointment of _____ as the new Managing Member for the above named Company is approved by the membership as of the date first written above. Additionally, it was **RESOLVED** and agreed by the Members that this new appointment shall become effective as of the date first written above.

There being no further business requiring member action or consideration, on a motion duly made, seconded and carried, the meeting was adjourned.

CERTIFICATION OF COMPANY SECRETARY

I the undersigned, certify that I am the duly appointed Secretary of the above named Company and that the forgoing Resolution is a true and accurate copy of a Resolution duly adopted at a meeting of the Members thereof, convened and held in accordance with the Operating Agreement of said Company and that the Resolution is now in full force and effect.

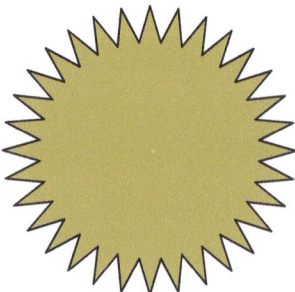

IN WITNESS THEREOF, I have affixed my name as Secretary of the above named Company and have attached the seal of said Company to this Resolution.

Dated _____ 20___

_____
Company Secretary

MINUTES OF A SPECIAL MEETING OF THE MEMBERS OF
(Replace This With The Name Of Your LLC)
A (Name of State) LIMITED LIABILITY COMPANY
FOR
USE OF PERSONAL CREDIT

The Secretary announced that pursuant to the Operating Agreement of the above named Limited Liability Company, a special meeting of the Members was held on the _____ day of _____, 20___ at _____ o'clock __M. The chairman then declared that the meeting was to be held in compliance with applicable statutes.

The chairman of the meeting then discussed having one or more of the Members of the above named Company use their personal credit and/or credit cards to facilitate the needs of the Company due to the fact that the Company while earning money, has no credit history (credit worthiness) and the Member(s) in question have credit worthiness but lack financial resources.

On motion duly made and carried, it was **RESOLVED** and **ORDERED** that the following individuals would be authorized to state the Company's income on any application for credit (intended for the use of the Company only) in conjunction with said Member's personal credit history in order to secure credit and/or credit cards to be primarily used for the benefit of this Company. In addition, it was **RESOLVED** and **ORDERED** that this Company shall directly pay (by check) all charges associated with the issuance of said credit/cards and/or the payment for any purchases using said credit/cards by this Company.

_____   _____
Printed Name   Signature

CERTIFICATION OF COMPANY SECRETARY

I the undersigned, certify that I am the duly appointed Secretary of the above named Company and that the forgoing Resolution is a true and accurate copy of a Resolution duly adopted at a meeting of the Members thereof, convened and held in accordance with the Operating Agreement of said Company and that the Resolution is now in full force and effect.

IN WITNESS THEREOF, I have affixed my name as Secretary of the above named Company and have attached the seal of said Company to this Resolution.

Dated _____ 20___

_____
Company Secretary

Asset Protection Services
of America

**Limited Partnership
Documents**

AssetProtectionServices.com

RESOLUTION OF PARTNERS OF
(Replace This With The Name Of Your LP)
A *(Name of State)* LIMITED PARTNERSHIP
TO
ACQUIRE ASSETS OF A BUSINESS

The General Partner announced that pursuant to the Partnership Agreement of the above named Limited Partnership, a special meeting of the Partners was held on the _____ day of _____, 20____ at _____ o'clock ___M. The chairman then declared that the meeting was to be held in compliance with applicable statutes.

WHEREAS, it is in the best interests of the Partnership to acquire the assets of the following entity as a going concern _____*(put in the business name)*.

It is hereby **RESOLVED**, that the Partnership execute an agreement to purchase the business assets of the above-stated entity as per the **Purchase Agreement** attached hereto; and

It is further **RESOLVED**, that the General Partner or other Partner of the Partnership named _____ be and is hereby authorized to execute such further documents and undertake such other acts as are reasonably required to carry out and conclude said transaction to purchase assets.

_____   _____
General Partner   General Partner

_____   _____
Partner   Partner

CERTIFICATION OF PARTNERSHIP GENERAL PARTNER

I the undersigned, certify that I am the duly appointed General Partner of the above named Partnership and that the forgoing Resolution is a true and accurate copy of a Resolution duly adopted at a meeting of the Partners thereof, convened and held in accordance with the Partnership Agreement of said Partnership and that the Resolution is now in full force and effect.

IN WITNESS THEREOF, I have affixed my name as General Partner of the above named Partnership and have attached the seal of said Partnership to this Resolution.

Dated _____ 20____

_____
Partnership General Partner

NOTICE OF MEETING OF PARTNERS OF
(Replace This With The Name Of Your LP)
A (Name of State) LIMITED PARTNERSHIP
TO
ADD NEW PARTNERS

The General Partner announced that pursuant to the Partnership Agreement of the above named Limited Partnership, a special meeting of the Partners was held on the _____ day of _____, 20___ at _____ o'clock __M. The chairman then declared that the meeting was to be held in compliance with applicable statutes.

The purpose of the meeting is to consider increasing the number of Partners of the Partnership and amending the limited partnership agreement in connection therewith.

This Notice given on this the _____ 20___, by a General Partner of the Partnership, by mailing a true and correct copy of this Notice to the address of each Partner of the Partnership at least 10 days prior to such meeting.

_____
General Partner

RESOLUTION OF PARTNERS OF
(Replace This With The Name Of Your LP)
A (Name of State) LIMITED PARTNERSHIP
FOR
ADDING NEW PARTNERS

The General Partner announced that pursuant to the Partnership Agreement of the above named Limited Partnership, a special meeting of the Partners was held on the _____ day of _____, 20____ at _____ o'clock ___M. The chairman then declared that the meeting was to be held in compliance with applicable statutes.

The purpose of the meeting was to consider increasing the number of partners of the Partnership and amending the partnership agreement in connection therewith.

Upon motion duly made and seconded, the Partners approved the following resolution:

RESOLVED, that the Partners of the Partnership are increased from _____ (____) to _____ (____) and the following persons are admitted as Partners subject to the condition below:

_____   _____
Partner   Partner

_____   _____
Partner   Partner

_____   _____
Partner   Partner

The Condition of their being admitted as Partners is:

_____

_____

_____

SO RESOLVED, There being no further business, the meeting was adjourned.

_____
General Partner

AMENDMENT TO
ARTICLES OF ORGANIZATION AND/OR PARTNERSHIP AGREEMENT
FOR
(Replace This With The Name Of Your LP)
A *(Name of State)* LIMITED PARTNERSHIP

There was presented to the Partners an amendment to the _____ Articles of organization / _____ Partnership Agreement for the Partnership. After consideration by the Partners of the Partnership, it was **RESOLVED,** that the following amendment be made:

_____

_____

_____

_____

_____

The General Partner shall amend the document, file the document with the proper state agencies, if necessary, and distribute the amended document to the partners of the partnership.

_____   _____
Partner   Partner

_____   _____
Partner   Partner

_____   _____
Partner   Partner

SO RESOLVED, There being no further business, the meeting was adjourned.

_____
General Partner

NOTICE OF MEETING OF PARTNERS OF
(Replace This With The Name Of Your LP)
A *(Name of State)* LIMITED PARTNERSHIP
FOR
ANNUAL DISBURSEMENTS TO PARTNERS

The General Partner announced that pursuant to the Partnership Agreement of the above named Limited Partnership, a special meeting of the Partners was held on the _____ day of _____, 20___ at _____ o'clock __M. The chairman then declared that the meeting was to be held in compliance with applicable statutes.

The purpose of the meeting is to consider annual disbursements to the Partners of the Partnership. At the meeting the Partnership proposes to seek disbursement to the Partners of the Partnership of _____ ($ _____) dollars in accordance with the Partnership Agreement of the Partnership to the following Partners:

_____   _____
Partners   Partners

_____   _____
Partners   Partners

_____   _____
Partners   Partners

This Notice given on this the _____ day of _____, 20___, by a General Partner of the Partnership, by mailing a true and correct copy of this Notice to the address of each Partner of the Partnership at least 10 days prior to such meeting.

_____
General Partner

RESOLUTION OF PARTNERS OF
(Replace This With The Name Of Your LP)
A (Name of State) LIMITED PARTNERSHIP
FOR
ANNUAL DISBURSEMENTS TO PARTNERS

The General Partner announced that pursuant to the Partnership Agreement of the above named Limited Partnership, a special meeting of the Partners was held on the _____ day of _____, 20___ at _____ o'clock __M. The chairman then declared that the meeting was to be held in compliance with applicable statutes.

RESOLVED, annual disbursements to the Partners of the Partnership shall be made as follows:

_____	$_____	_____	$_____
Partner	Amount	Partner	Amount

_____	$_____	_____	$_____
Partner	Amount	Partner	Amount

_____	$_____	_____	$_____
Partner	Amount	Partner	Amount

_____ $_____
General Partner   Amount

SO RESOLVED, there being no further business, the meeting was adjourned.

_____   _____
Partner   Partner

_____   _____
Partner   Partner

_____   _____
Partner   Partner

_____
General Partner

MINUTES OF THE ANNUAL MEETING OF PARTNERS
OF
(Replace This With The Name Of Your LP)
A *(Name of State)* LIMITED PARTNERSHIP

The General Partner announced that pursuant to the Partnership Agreement of the above named Limited Partnership, a special meeting of the Partners was held on the _____ day of _____, 20___ at _____ o'clock __M. The chairman then declared that the meeting was to be held in compliance with applicable statutes.

The Partners, fixing such time and place and prefixed to the minutes of this meeting, were present at the meeting all of the Partners of the above named Limited Partnership.

_____   _____
Partner   Partner

_____   _____
Partner   Partner

_____   _____
Partner   Partner

The meeting was called to order by _____ it was moved, seconded and unanimously carried that _____ act as Chairman and that _____ act as General Partner.

The Chairman then stated that all of the Partners were present. The General Partner presented his/hers annual report and, after discussion, the report was accepted and ordered filed with the general partner.

The Chairman noted that it was in order to consider electing general partners for the ensuing year. Upon nominations duly made and seconded, the following were unanimously elected General Partners of the Limited Partnership, to serve for the ensuing year and until their successors are elected and qualified:

General Partner: _____

General Partner: _____

CERTIFICATION OF PARTNERSHIP GENERAL PARTNER

I the undersigned, certify that I am the duly appointed General Partner of the above named Partnership and that the forgoing Resolution is a true and accurate copy of a Resolution duly adopted at a meeting of the Partners thereof, convened and held in accordance with the Partnership Agreement of said Partnership and that the Resolution is now in full force and effect.

IN WITNESS THEREOF, I have affixed my name as General Partner of the above named Partnership and have attached the seal of said Partnership to this Resolution.

Dated _____ 20____

_____
Partnership General Partner

_____
Partner

_____
Partner

_____
Partner

_____
Partner

_____
Partner

_____
Partner

WE, the undersigned, being all of the Partners of the Partnership, hereby agree and consent that the annual meeting of Partners of the Partnership be held on the date and time and at the place designated hereunder, and do hereby waive all notice whatsoever of such meeting and of any adjournment or adjournments thereof.

We do agree and consent that any and all lawful business may be transacted at such meeting or at any adjournment or adjournments thereof as may be deemed advisable by the Partners present thereat. Any business transacted at such meeting or at any adjournment or adjournments thereof shall be as valid and legal and of the same force and effect as if such meeting or adjourned meeting were held after notice.

Place of Meeting: _____

Date of Meeting: _____

Time of Meeting: _____

Purpose of Meeting:_____

General Partner: _____

General Partner: _____

Partner: _____

Partner: _____

Partner: _____

Partner: _____

APPROVAL OF TRANSACTION BENEFITING PARTNERS
FOR
(Replace This With The Name Of Your LP)
A *(Name of State)* LIMITED PARTNERSHIP

There was presented to the Partners the following transaction:

_____

_____

_____

_____

_____

The transaction has a potential benefit to one or more Partners of the Partnership. After consideration by the Partners of the Partnership, it is hereby **RESOLVED,** that the above-described transaction has been approved.

_____   _____
Partner   Partner

_____   _____
Partner   Partner

_____   _____
Partner   Partner

ASSIGNMENT OF PARTNER INTEREST
IN
(Replace This With The Name Of Your LP)
A *(Name of State)* LIMITED PARTNERSHIP

For Valuable Consideration, the receipt and sufficient of which, is herby acknowledged, I the undersigned "Assignor", Partner of the above named Limited Partnership, hereinafter "Partnership", does hereby assign, transfer and warrant to _____, "Assignee", all of Partners ownership interest in the Partnership.

Except as otherwise provided in the partnership agreement, a Partnership interest in a Limited Partnership is assignable in whole or in part. The Partnership Agreement of the Partnership does not prohibit assignment of a Partnership interest. An Assignment of this interest does not dissolve the Partnership or entitle the Assignee to become or to exercise any rights of a Partner. An assignment entitles the Assignee to receive, to the extent assigned, the distributions of cash and other property and the allocations of profits, losses, income, gains, deductions, credits, or similar items to which the Assignee's Assignor would have been entitled. The Assignor ceases to be a Partner upon assignment of all the Assignor's membership interest. Except as provided herein, until Assignee becomes a Partner, the Assignee does not have liability as a Partner solely because of the assignment.

Assignee may become a Partner if and to the extent that the Assignor gives the Assignee that right and either of the following occurs:

1. The Assignor has been given the authority in writing in the Partnership Agreement to give an Assignee the right to become a Partner.

2. All other Partners consent.

By execution hereof, Assignor, gives to Assignee the right to become a Partner of the Partnership. Once Assignee becomes a Partner, he has to the extent assigned the rights and powers of a Partner under the Partnership Agreement are subject to the restrictions and liabilities of a Partner under the Partnership Agreement. Assignee is liable for the obligations of Assignor to make contributions as provided by law. Assignee is not obligated for liabilities hat could not be ascertained from a written Partnership Agreement and that were unknown to Assignee at the time he becomes a partner.

Assignor is not released from his liability to a Limited Partnership for the past capital contributions required by law whether or not the Assignee becomes a Partner.

Dated This _____, 20____

_____
Partner

RESOLUTION OF THE PARTNERS OF
(Replace This With The Name Of Your LP)
A *(Name of State)* LIMITED PARTNERSHIP
FOR
BILL OF SALE & AGREEMENT

The General Partner announced that pursuant to the Partnership Agreement of the above named Limited Partnership, a special meeting of the Partners was held on the _____ day of _____, 20____ at _____ o'clock ___M. The chairman then declared that the meeting was to be held in compliance with applicable statutes.

The purpose of the meeting was to consider the purchase all rights, title and interest in the property and assets shown on **ATTACHMENT "A"** that must be attached hereto and thereby made a part hereof.

In return for the transfer of said property, the Partnership agrees to assume, pay and discharge all debts, duties and obligations that exist as of the date of transfer to this Partnership. Further, the Partnership agrees to indemnify and hold transferor free from any liability for any such debts, duties and obligations, suits, actions, or legal proceedings brought to enforce or collect such debt, duty or obligation.

In addition, appoints the Partnership to do all things allowed by law to demand, receive, and collect for itself any debt or obligation now owing and authorizes it to recover and collect any such debt or obligation and to use the name(s) of transferor in such manner as it considers necessary to collect and recover such debts or obligations

CERTIFICATION OF PARTNERSHIP GENERAL PARTNER

I the undersigned, certify that I am the duly appointed General Partner of the above named Partnership and that the forgoing Resolution is a true and accurate copy of a Resolution duly adopted at a meeting of the Partners thereof, convened and held in accordance with the Partnership Agreement of said Partnership and that the Resolution is now in full force and effect.

IN WITNESS THEREOF, I have affixed my name as General Partner of the above named Partnership and have attached the seal of said Partnership to this Resolution.

Dated _____ 20____

_____
Partnership General Partner

_____

The General Partner announced that pursuant to the Partnership Agreement of the above named Limited Partnership, a special meeting of the Partners was held on the _____ day of _____, 20___ at _____ o'clock ___M. The chairman then declared that the meeting was to be held in compliance with applicable statutes.

The chairman of the meeting then discussed:

_____

_____

_____

On motion duly made and carried, it was **RESOLVED** and **ORDERED** that:

_____

_____

_____

CERTIFICATION OF PARTNERSHIP GENERAL PARTNER

I the undersigned, certify that I am the duly appointed General Partner of the above named Partnership and that the forgoing Resolution is a true and accurate copy of a Resolution duly adopted at a meeting of the Partners thereof, convened and held in accordance with the Partnership Agreement of said Partnership and that the Resolution is now in full force and effect.

IN WITNESS THEREOF, I have affixed my name as General Partner of the above named Partnership and have attached the seal of said Partnership to this Resolution.

Dated _____ 20___

_____
Partnership General Partner

RESOLUTION OF THE PARTNERS OF
(Replace This With The Name Of Your LP)
A *(Name of State)* LIMITED PARTNERSHIP
TO
BORROW CAPITAL

The General Partner announced that pursuant to the Partnership Agreement of the above named Limited Partnership, a special meeting of the Partners was held on the _____ day of _____, 20____ at _____ o'clock __M. The chairman then declared that the meeting was to be held in compliance with applicable statutes.

WHEREAS, the Partnership is in need of additional capital, and

WHEREAS, _____, _____ as a Partners of the Partnership, has agreed to loan to the Partnership the sum of _____
($ _____), and

WHEREAS, such borrowing appears to be advantageous to the Partnership as it is on better terms than would be available elsewhere; be it: **RESOLVED** and **ORDERED**, that the Partnership borrow the sum of _____ ($ _____), from the above named Partner and that said sum be repaid in or within _____ (____) years with interest thereon at _____ (_____%) on the unpaid balance, all as more fully set forth in a promissory note and collateral loan documents that when executed, must be placed in the minutes of this Partnership.

CERTIFICATION OF PARTNERSHIP GENERAL PARTNER

I the undersigned, certify that I am the duly appointed General Partner of the above named Partnership and that the forgoing Resolution is a true and accurate copy of a Resolution duly adopted at a meeting of the Partners thereof, convened and held in accordance with the Partnership Agreement of said Partnership and that the Resolution is now in full force and effect.

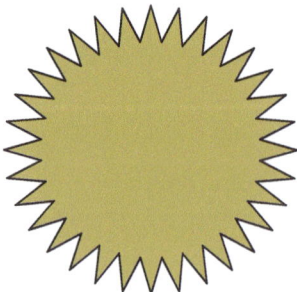

IN WITNESS THEREOF, I have affixed my name as General Partner of the above named Partnership and have attached the seal of said Partnership to this Resolution.

Dated _____ 20____

_____
Partnership General Partner

RESOLUTION OF THE PARTNERS OF
(Replace This With The Name Of Your LP)
A *(Name of State)* LIMITED PARTNERSHIP
TO
BORROW ON ACCOUNTS RECEIVABLE, EQUIPMENT, INVENTORY

The General Partner announced that pursuant to the Partnership Agreement of the above named Limited Partnership, a special meeting of the Partners was held on the _____ day of _____, 20____ at _____ o'clock ___M. The chairman then declared that the meeting was to be held in compliance with applicable statutes.

RESOLVED and **ORDERED**, that the Partner of this Partnership, is hereby authorized and directed to borrow the sum of _____ ($ _____), from any entity or individual on the terms set out in a contract or Promissory Note which when executed must be placed in the minutes of this meeting and to execute a mortgage in favor of the Lender covering the accounts receivable, equipment, fixtures, furniture, inventory or merchandise set out in a Schedule attached to the minutes of this meeting.

Therefore, it is **FURTHER RESOLVED** and **ORDERED**, that the Partner of the Partnership is hereby authorized and directed to provide for creditors of the Partnership all notices required by law to be given to the creditors of the Partnership, and to do everything else that may be necessary to complete the authorized transaction.

CERTIFICATION OF PARTNERSHIP GENERAL PARTNER

I the undersigned, certify that I am the duly appointed General Partner of the above named Partnership and that the forgoing Resolution is a true and accurate copy of a Resolution duly adopted at a meeting of the Partners thereof, convened and held in accordance with the Partnership Agreement of said Partnership and that the Resolution is now in full force and effect.

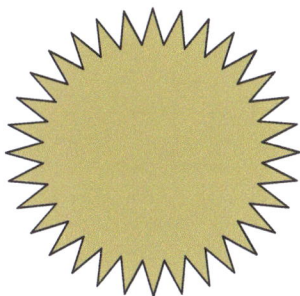

IN WITNESS THEREOF, I have affixed my name as General Partner of the above named Partnership and have attached the seal of said Partnership to this Resolution.

Dated _____ 20____

_____
Partnership General Partner

CAPITAL CONTRIBUTION OF PARTNERS
OF
(Replace This With The Name Of Your LP)
A *(Name of State)* LIMITED PARTNERSHIP
AS OF _____, 20____

*(**NOTE:** Capital contributions can be cash or the value of providing services, property, equipment, supplies, etc.)*

(1) Partner's Name: _____

Complete Address: _____

_____

Capital Contribution: $_____

Percentage Interest: _____ (_____%)

(2) Partner's Name: _____

Complete Address: _____

_____

Capital Contribution: $_____

Percentage Interest: _____ (_____%)

(3) Partner's Name: _____

Complete Address: _____

_____

Capital Contribution: $_____

Percentage Interest: _____ (_____%)

(4) Partner's Name: _____

    Complete Address: _____

    _____

    Capital Contribution: $_____

    Percentage Interest: _____ (_____%)

(5) Partner's Name: _____

    Complete Address: _____

    _____

    Capital Contribution: $_____

    Percentage Interest: _____ (_____%)

(6) Partner's Name: _____

    Complete Address: _____

    _____

    Capital Contribution: $_____

    Percentage Interest: _____ (_____%)

(7) Partner's Name: _____

    Complete Address: _____

    _____

    Capital Contribution: $_____

    Percentage Interest: _____ (_____%)

CONSENT TO ACTION BY
GENERAL PARTNERS / PARTNERS
WITHOUT A MEETING
FOR
(Replace This With The Name Of Your LP)
A *(Name of State)* LIMITED PARTNERSHIP

By signing this document, the undersigned, which are all of the _____ General Partners / _____ Partners of the above named Partnership, consent to the taking of the following actions without a meeting of the General Partners or Partners in accordance with the terms of the Partnership Agreement of the Partnership:

RESOLVED, that _____ is elected to serve as a General Partner of the Partnership for a term beginning on the date of this consent to action and ending at the next meeting of Partners of the Partnership called for the purpose of electing General Partners, or the General Partner's death, resignation, or removal, if earlier.

RESOLVED, that

_____

_____

_____

is authorized and the above named General Partner is hereby directed to do all things necessary to complete the transaction herein above discussed.

The actions taken will be effective when this Consent to Action has been singed by all _____ General Partners / _____ Partners of the Company.

_____   _____
Partner   Partner

_____   _____
Partner   Partner

_____   _____
Partner   Partner

_____   _____
General Partner   General Partner

MINUTES OF A SPECIAL MEETING OF THE PARTNERS
(Replace This With The Name Of Your LP)
A (Name of State) LIMITED PARTNERSHIP
TO
DEMISE OR INCAPACITATION OF PARTNERS

The General Partner announced that pursuant to the Partnership Agreement of the above named Limited Partnership, a special meeting of the Partners was held on the _____ day of _____, 20___ at _____ o'clock __M. The chairman then declared that the meeting was to be held in compliance with applicable statutes.

The chairman of the meeting then discussed electing assistant Partner who shall immediately replace their respective elected Partners in case of the demise or incapacitation of any or all of the current Partners of this Partnership pursuant to the Partnership Agreement of this Partnership. On motion duly made and carried, it was **RESOLVED** and **ORDERED** that the following individual be elected and has accepted the respective office at the meeting:

ASSISTANT PARTNER: _____

The chairman of the meeting then discussed electing substitute signatories on any and all Partnership bank accounts and merchant accounts for this Partnership in case of the demise or incapacitation of any or all of the current signatories of this Partnership. On motion duly made and carried, it was; **RESOLVED** and **ORDERED** that the following individual be elected as substitute signatories on any and all company bank accounts and merchant accounts for this Partnership in case of the demise or incapacitation of any or all of the current signatories of this Partnership and each has accepted their respective offices at the meeting:

_____   _____
Printed Name   Signature

CERTIFICATION OF PARTNERSHIP GENERAL PARTNER

I the undersigned, certify that I am the duly appointed General Partner of the above named Partnership and that the forgoing Resolution is a true and accurate copy of a Resolution duly adopted at a meeting of the Partners thereof, convened and held in accordance with the Partnership Agreement of said Partnership and that the Resolution is now in full force and effect.

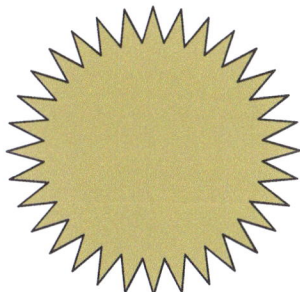

IN WITNESS THEREOF, I have affixed my name as General Partner of the above named Partnership and have attached the seal of said Partnership to this Resolution.

Dated _____ 20___

_____
Partnership General Partner

RESOLUTION OF
(Replace This With The Name Of Your LP)
A *(Name of State)* LIMITED PARTNERSHIP
FOR
DISSOLUTION OF LIMITED PARTNERSHIP

The General Partner announced that pursuant to the Partnership Agreement of the above named Limited Partnership, a special meeting of the Partners was held on the _____ day of _____, 20___ at _____ o'clock __M. The chairman then declared that the meeting was to be held in compliance with applicable statutes.

RESOLVED that _____ shall dissolve forthwith, and it is:

FURTHER RESOLVED and **ORDERED**, that the General Partner of the Partnership is hereby authorized and directed to file the necessary Certificate of Dissolution of this Limited Partnership with Secretary of State in accordance with the laws of the State of _____.

CERTIFICATION OF PARTNERSHIP GENERAL PARTNER

I the undersigned, certify that I am the duly appointed General Partner of the above named Partnership and that the forgoing Resolution is a true and accurate copy of a Resolution duly adopted at a meeting of the Partners thereof, convened and held in accordance with the Partnership Agreement of said Partnership and that the Resolution is now in full force and effect.

IN WITNESS THEREOF, I have affixed my name as General Partner of the above named Partnership and have attached the seal of said Partnership to this Resolution.

Dated _____ 20___

_____
Partnership General Partner

RESOLUTION OF THE PARTNERS OF
(Replace This With The Name Of Your LP)
A *(Name of State)* LIMITED PARTNERSHIP
TO
LOAN FUNDS TO PARTNER

The General Partner announced that pursuant to the Partnership Agreement of the above named Limited Partnership, a special meeting of the Partners was held on the _____ day of _____, 20____ at _____ o'clock ___M. The chairman then declared that the meeting was to be held in compliance with applicable statutes.

WHEREAS, _____ a Partner of this Partnership, has requested of this Partnership an advance and/or loan in the amount of _____ ($ _____), together with interest, and

WHEREAS, the Partnership has adequate financial resources to make such loan without impairing its growth or profitability, and that said loan is deemed reasonably secure and in the best interests of the Partnership to make, be it **RESOLVED** and **ORDERED**, that the Partnership issue a loan to _____ in the amount of _____ ($ _____), to be repaid within _____ (____) months with interest of _____ (_____%) on the unpaid balance, and that the borrower execute to the Partnership a promissory note evidencing said indebtedness.

CERTIFICATION OF PARTNERSHIP GENERAL PARTNER

I the undersigned, certify that I am the duly appointed General Partner of the above named Partnership and that the forgoing Resolution is a true and accurate copy of a Resolution duly adopted at a meeting of the Partners thereof, convened and held in accordance with the Partnership Agreement of said Partnership and that the Resolution is now in full force and effect.

IN WITNESS THEREOF, I have affixed my name as General Partner of the above named Partnership and have attached the seal of said Partnership to this Resolution.

Dated _____ 20____

_____
Partnership General Partner

MEETING PARTICIPANT LIST
FOR
(Replace This With The Name Of Your LP)
A *(Name of State)* LIMITED PARTNERSHIP

Type of Meeting: _____ Regular; or

    _____ Special

Meeting of: _____ General Partners; and/or

    _____ Partners

Date: _____ 20____   Time: 3:00 p.m.

Meetings Participants: General Partner: _____

    General Partner: _____

    Partner: _____

    Partner: _____

    Partner: _____

    Partner: _____

RESOLUTION OF THE PARTNERS OF
(Replace This With The Name Of Your LP)
A (Name of State) LIMITED PARTNERSHIP
TO
PURCHASE EQUIPMENT

The General Partner announced that pursuant to the Partnership Agreement of the above named Limited Partnership, a special meeting of the Partners was held on the _____ day of _____, 20___ at _____ o'clock __M. The chairman then declared that the meeting was to be held in compliance with applicable statutes.

WHEREAS, certain equipment is necessary for the operation of the business, therefore be it **RESOLVED** and **ORDERED**, that this Partnership shall purchase the following equipment:

Description: _____

Model Number: _____

Purchase From: _____

Purchase Price: $_____

To be paid: _____ Day _____ Week _____ Month

_____ Other _____

CERTIFICATION OF PARTNERSHIP GENERAL PARTNER

I the undersigned, certify that I am the duly appointed General Partner of the above named Partnership and that the forgoing Resolution is a true and accurate copy of a Resolution duly adopted at a meeting of the Partners thereof, convened and held in accordance with the Partnership Agreement of said Partnership and that the Resolution is now in full force and effect.

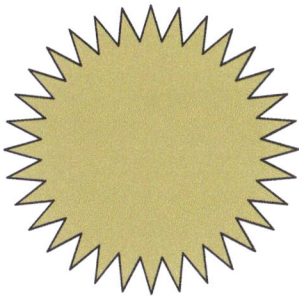

IN WITNESS THEREOF, I have affixed my name as General Partner of the above named Partnership and have attached the seal of said Partnership to this Resolution.

Dated _____ 20___

_____
Partnership General Partner

RESOLUTION OF THE PARTNERS OF
(Replace This With The Name Of Your LP)
A (Name of State) LIMITED PARTNERSHIP
TO
PURCHASE MOTOR VEHICLES

The General Partner announced that pursuant to the Partnership Agreement of the above named Limited Partnership, a special meeting of the Partners was held on the _____ day of _____, 20____ at _____ o'clock ___M. The chairman then declared that the meeting was to be held in compliance with applicable statutes.

WHEREAS, motor vehicles are necessary for the operation of the business, therefore be it **RESOLVED** and **ORDERED**, that this Partnership shall purchase the motor vehicle(s) described as:

Description: _____

Model Number: _____

Lease/Rent From: _____

Lease/Rental price: $_____

To be paid: _____ Day _____ Week _____ Month

_____ Other _____

CERTIFICATION OF PARTNERSHIP GENERAL PARTNER

I the undersigned, certify that I am the duly appointed General Partner of the above named Partnership and that the forgoing Resolution is a true and accurate copy of a Resolution duly adopted at a meeting of the Partners thereof, convened and held in accordance with the Partnership Agreement of said Partnership and that the Resolution is now in full force and effect.

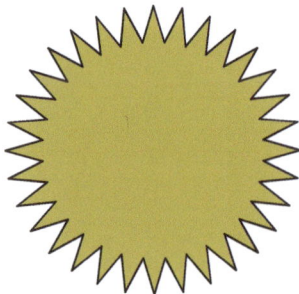

IN WITNESS THEREOF, I have affixed my name as General Partner of the above named Partnership and have attached the seal of said Partnership to this Resolution.

Dated _____ 20____

_____
Partnership General Partner

RESOLUTION OF THE PARTNERS OF
(Replace This With The Name Of Your LP)
A *(Name of State)* LIMITED PARTNERSHIP
FOR
PURCHASE REAL PROPERTY

The General Partner announced that pursuant to the Partnership Agreement of the above named Limited Partnership, a special meeting of the Partners was held on the _____ day of _____, 20____ at _____ o'clock ___M. The chairman then declared that the meeting was to be held in compliance with applicable statutes.

WHEREAS, the Partnership has decided to purchase various parcels of real estate under the terms of the attached **Real Estate Purchase Services Agreement**.

Therefore, be it: **RESOLVED** and **ORDERED**, that the Partnership purchase and acquire said real estate as set forth in the Real Estate Purchase Services Agreement as annexed hereto and that the named Authorized Signatory be authorized to represent this Partnership as the signatory for any and all documentary requirements pertaining thereto.

There being no further business requiring Partners action or consideration, and on a motion duly made, seconded and carried, the meeting was adjourned.

CERTIFICATION OF PARTNERSHIP GENERAL PARTNER

I the undersigned, certify that I am the duly appointed General Partner of the above named Partnership and that the forgoing Resolution is a true and accurate copy of a Resolution duly adopted at a meeting of the Partners thereof, convened and held in accordance with the Partnership Agreement of said Partnership and that the Resolution is now in full force and effect.

IN WITNESS THEREOF, I have affixed my name as General Partner of the above named Partnership and have attached the seal of said Partnership to this Resolution.

Dated _____ 20____

_____
Partnership General Partner

RESOLUTION OF
(Replace This With The Name Of Your LP)
A *(Name of State)* LIMITED PARTNERSHIP
FOR
ESTABLISHING THE AUTHORIZED SIGNATORY FOR THE
PURCHASE AND/OR SALE OF REAL PROPERTY

The General Partner announced that pursuant to the Partnership Agreement of the above named Limited Partnership, a special meeting of the Partners was held on the _____ day of _____, 20___ at _____ o'clock ___M. The chairman then declared that the meeting was to be held in compliance with applicable statutes.

The chairman of the meeting then discussed granting full signatory authority to the named Authorized Signatory to sign any and all banking documents or instruments, contracts and/or any other documents as needed on behalf of this Partnership. On motion duly made and carried, it was, **RESOLVED** and **ORDERED** that the named Authorized Signatory be henceforth granted the full signatory authority and power to grant, bargain, convey, sell, acquire or purchase; to sign promissory notes, mortgages or deeds of trust encumbering the property of this Partnership; to contract for the sale, conveyance, acquisition or purchase of any and all property belonging to this Partnership; to execute escrow instructions, trust agreements, agreements for sale, deeds or other conveyances of land, bills of sale, construction contracts, leases, subordinate agreements subordinating any lien, encumbrance or other right in real or personal property to any other lien or encumbrance or other contracts and/or instrument(s) necessary to effect such sale, conveyance, exchange, acquisition or purchase and to give warrantees to the purchasers thereof; to execute any and all documents deemed necessary without the attestation of the general partners or affixing of the Partnership seal thereto and upon execution of such instruments by the named Authorized Signatory, such documents so executed shall be valid and binding without further act or specific resolution of the General Partners.

CERTIFICATION OF PARTNERSHIP GENERAL PARTNER

I the undersigned, certify that I am the duly appointed General Partner of the above named Partnership and that the forgoing Resolution is a true and accurate copy of a Resolution duly adopted at a meeting of the Partners thereof, convened and held in accordance with the Partnership Agreement of said Partnership and that the Resolution is now in full force and effect.

IN WITNESS THEREOF, I have affixed my name as General Partner of the above named Partnership and have attached the seal of said Partnership to this Resolution.

Dated _____ 20___

_____
Partnership General Partner

RESOLUTION OF THE PARTNERS OF
(Replace This With The Name Of Your LP)
A *(Name of State)* LIMITED PARTNERSHIP
FOR
RENT/LEASE EQUIPMENT

The General Partner announced that pursuant to the Partnership Agreement of the above named Limited Partnership, a special meeting of the Partners was held on the _____ day of _____, 20____ at _____ o'clock __M. The chairman then declared that the meeting was to be held in compliance with applicable statutes.

WHEREAS, certain equipment is necessary for the operation of the business, therefore be it **RESOLVED** and **ORDERED**, that this Partnership shall rent or lease the following equipment:

Year, Make and Model: _____

License Number _____

V.I.N. _____

Lease/Rent From: _____

Lease/Rental price: $_____

To be paid in: _____ CASH _____ CREDIT _____ OTHER:_____

CERTIFICATION OF PARTNERSHIP GENERAL PARTNER

I the undersigned, certify that I am the duly appointed General Partner of the above named Partnership and that the forgoing Resolution is a true and accurate copy of a Resolution duly adopted at a meeting of the Partners thereof, convened and held in accordance with the Partnership Agreement of said Partnership and that the Resolution is now in full force and effect.

IN WITNESS THEREOF, I have affixed my name as General Partner of the above named Partnership and have attached the seal of said Partnership to this Resolution.

Dated _____ 20____

_____
Partnership General Partner

RESOLUTION OF
(Replace This With The Name Of Your LP)
A *(Name of State)* LIMITED PARTNERSHIP
TO
RENT/LEASE HOME OR OFFICE

The General Partner announced that pursuant to the Partnership Agreement of the above named Limited Partnership, a special meeting of the Partners was held on the _____ day of _____, 20___ at _____ o'clock __M. The chairman then declared that the meeting was to be held in compliance with applicable statutes.

WHEREAS, it is necessary for the operation of the business of this Partnership to have an office location with living quarters in order for a Partner of this Partnership to protect the property of this Partnership and to be able to undertake the business of the above named Partnership regardless of the hour day or night. Therefore be it **RESOLVED** and **ORDERED** that this Partnership shall rent or lease the following location pursuant to the attached lease agreement (in the Partnership name).

Office Location (Description): _____

Address: _____

Leased/Rented From (Land Lord): _____

Address: _____

There being no further business requiring Partner action or consideration, and on a motion duly made, seconded and carried, the meeting was adjourned.

CERTIFICATION OF PARTNERSHIP GENERAL PARTNER

I the undersigned, certify that I am the duly appointed General Partner of the above named Partnership and that the forgoing Resolution is a true and accurate copy of a Resolution duly adopted at a meeting of the Partners thereof, convened and held in accordance with the Partnership Agreement of said Partnership and that the Resolution is now in full force and effect.

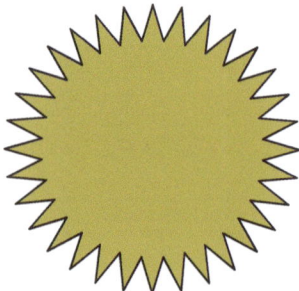

IN WITNESS THEREOF, I have affixed my name as General Partner of the above named Partnership and have attached the seal of said Partnership to this Resolution.

Dated _____ 20___

_____
Partnership General Partner

RESOLUTION OF
(Replace This With The Name Of Your LP)
A *(Name of State)* LIMITED PARTNERSHIP
TO
RENT/LEASE MOTOR VEHICLES

The General Partner announced that pursuant to the Partnership Agreement of the above named Limited Partnership, a special meeting of the Partners was held on the _____ day of _____, 20____ at _____ o'clock ___M. The chairman then declared that the meeting was to be held in compliance with applicable statutes.

WHEREAS, certain vehicles are necessary for the operation of the business, therefore be it **RESOLVED** and **ORDERED**, that this partnership shall rent or lease the following vehicles:

Year, Make and Model: _____

License Number: _____

V.I.N. _____

Purchase From: _____

Purchase price of: $_____

To be paid in: _____ Cash _____ Credit _____ Other:_____

CERTIFICATION OF PARTNERSHIP GENERAL PARTNER

I the undersigned, certify that I am the duly appointed General Partner of the above named Partnership and that the forgoing Resolution is a true and accurate copy of a Resolution duly adopted at a meeting of the Partners thereof, convened and held in accordance with the Partnership Agreement of said Partnership and that the Resolution is now in full force and effect.

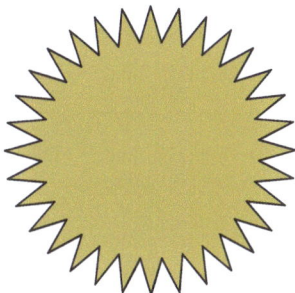

IN WITNESS THEREOF, I have affixed my name as General Partner of the above named Partnership and have attached the seal of said Partnership to this Resolution.

Dated _____ 20____

_____
Partnership General Partner

NOTICE OF MEETING OF PARTNERS OF
(Replace This With The Name Of Your LP)
A *(Name of State)* LIMITED PARTNERSHIP
RESIGNATION AND REPLACEMENT
OF GENERAL PARTNER

The General Partner announced that pursuant to the Partnership Agreement of the above named Limited Partnership, a special meeting of the Partners was held on the _____ day of _____, 20___ at _____ o'clock __M. The chairman then declared that the meeting was to be held in compliance with applicable statutes.

The Purpose of acceptance of the resignation of the General Partner and to appoint a new General Partner. Further to the resignation of _____ as the General Partner is hereby accepted and the appointment of _____ as the new General Partner has been approved and accepted by _____ on the date first written above.

This Notice given on this the _____ day of _____, 20___, by a General Partner, by mailing a true and correct copy of this Notice to the address of each Partner of the Partnership.

_____
General Partner

CERTIFICATION OF PARTNERSHIP GENERAL PARTNER

I the undersigned, certify that I am the duly appointed General Partner of the above named Partnership and that the forgoing Resolution is a true and accurate copy of a Resolution duly adopted at a meeting of the Partners thereof, convened and held in accordance with the Partnership Agreement of said Partnership and that the Resolution is now in full force and effect.

IN WITNESS THEREOF, I have affixed my name as General Partner of the above named Partnership and have attached the seal of said Partnership to this Resolution.

Dated _____ 20___

_____
Partnership General Partner

RESOLUTION OF PARTNERS OF
(Replace This With The Name Of Your LP)
A *(Name of State)* LIMITED PARTNERSHIP
FOR
SETTING GENERAL PARTNER SALARY

The General Partner announced that pursuant to the Partnership Agreement of the above named Limited Partnership, a special meeting of the Partners was held on the _____ day of _____, 20____ at _____ o'clock ___M. The chairman then declared that the meeting was to be held in compliance with applicable statutes.

WHEREAS, the Partnership desires to fill the position of General Partner for the yearly gross salary of _____ ($_____) with all usual deductions and benefits;

It is hereby **RESOLVED**, that _____ (***put in the person's name***) be entered on the payroll records of the Partnership with salary stated above.

The salary of any General Partner shall not commence until such time as the Partnership is profitable so as not to place the Partnership into financial distress by paying such salary.

_____   _____
Partner   Partner

_____   _____
Partner   Partner

_____   _____
Partner   Partner

CERTIFICATION OF PARTNERSHIP GENERAL PARTNER

I the undersigned, certify that I am the duly appointed General Partner of the above named Partnership and that the forgoing Resolution is a true and accurate copy of a Resolution duly adopted at a meeting of the Partners thereof, convened and held in accordance with the Partnership Agreement of said Partnership and that the Resolution is now in full force and effect.

IN WITNESS THEREOF, I have affixed my name as General Partner of the above named Partnership and have attached the seal of said Partnership to this Resolution.

Dated _____ 20____

_____
Partnership General Partner

RESOLUTION OF THE PARTNERS OF
(Replace This With The Name Of Your LP)
A *(Name of State)* LIMITED PARTNERSHIP
FOR
AUTHORIZE SALE/LEASEBACK TRANSACTION

The General Partner announced that pursuant to the Partnership Agreement of the above named Limited Partnership, a special meeting of the Partners was held on the _____ day of _____, 20____ at _____ o'clock ___M. The chairman then declared that the meeting was to be held in compliance with applicable statutes.

The purpose of the meeting was to consider the advisability for the Partnership to raise capital through a sale/leaseback of certain of its assets. Therefore, be it **RESOLVED** and **ORDERED**, that the Partnership sell and lease back the following property to the highest "bidder":

Description: _____

_____

_____

Sale price: $_____

And that concurrently the Partnership execute a lease for said property for a period of _____ (___) years at a net annual rental not to exceed _____ (____%), (percent) of the sales price, all in accord with generally prevailing sales/leaseback terms.

CERTIFICATION OF PARTNERSHIP GENERAL PARTNER

I the undersigned, certify that I am the duly appointed General Partner of the above named Partnership and that the forgoing Resolution is a true and accurate copy of a Resolution duly adopted at a meeting of the Partners thereof, convened and held in accordance with the Partnership Agreement of said Partnership and that the Resolution is now in full force and effect.

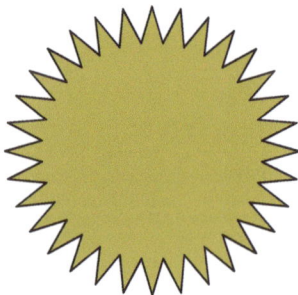

IN WITNESS THEREOF, I have affixed my name as General Partner of the above named Partnership and have attached the seal of said Partnership to this Resolution.

Dated _____ 20____

_____
Partnership General Partner

RESOLUTION OF THE PARTNERS OF
(Replace This With The Name Of Your LP)
A *(Name of State)* LIMITED PARTNERSHIP
TO
SELL PARTNERSHIP PROPERTY

The General Partner announced that pursuant to the Partnership Agreement of the above named Limited Partnership, a special meeting of the Partners was held on the _____ day of _____, 20____ at _____ o'clock ___M. The chairman then declared that the meeting was to be held in compliance with applicable statutes.

RESOLVED, that the General Partners of this Partnership are authorized to sell or exchange all or any part of this Partnership's property and assets, whether personal, tangible or intangible, including goodwill, upon such terms and conditions as the General Partners shall determine are in the best interests of the Partnership.

CERTIFICATION OF PARTNERSHIP GENERAL PARTNER

I the undersigned, certify that I am the duly appointed General Partner of the above named Partnership and that the forgoing Resolution is a true and accurate copy of a Resolution duly adopted at a meeting of the Partners thereof, convened and held in accordance with the Partnership Agreement of said Partnership and that the Resolution is now in full force and effect.

IN WITNESS THEREOF, I have affixed my name as General Partner of the above named Partnership and have attached the seal of said Partnership to this Resolution.

Dated _____ 20____

_____
Partnership General Partner

RESOLUTION OF THE PARTNERS OF
(Replace This With The Name Of Your LP)
A (Name of State) LIMITED PARTNERSHIP
TO
SELL REAL PROPERTY

The General Partner announced that pursuant to the Partnership Agreement of the above named Limited Partnership, a special meeting of the Partners was held on the _____ day of _____, 20___ at _____ o'clock __M. The chairman then declared that the meeting was to be held in compliance with applicable statutes.

WHEREAS, the Partnership is in need of additional capital, and

WHEREAS, the Partnership owns certain real estate that is no longer needed and that it would further be desirous to sell some; be it;

RESOLVED, that the Partnership sell real estate known or described as _____ in the city of _____, county of _____, state of _____ for the most advantageous return to the Partnership, as further set forth in a sales agreement as annexed hereto.

Further, it is **RESOLVED** and **ORDERED**, that the General Partner of this Partnership be instructed to locate a suitable buyer for said sale and to execute all required documents for it.

CERTIFICATION OF PARTNERSHIP GENERAL PARTNER

I the undersigned, certify that I am the duly appointed General Partner of the above named Partnership and that the forgoing Resolution is a true and accurate copy of a Resolution duly adopted at a meeting of the Partners thereof, convened and held in accordance with the Partnership Agreement of said Partnership and that the Resolution is now in full force and effect.

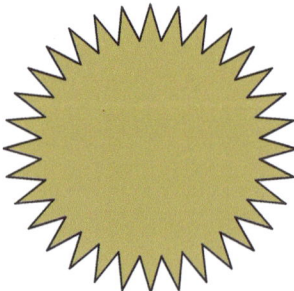

IN WITNESS THEREOF, I have affixed my name as General Partner of the above named Partnership and have attached the seal of said Partnership to this Resolution.

Dated _____ 20___

_____
Partnership General Partner

RESOLUTION OF THE PARTNERS OF
(Replace This With The Name Of Your LP)
A *(Name of State)* LIMITED PARTNERSHIP
FOR
AUTHORIZED SIGNATORY FOR PARTNERSHIP

The General Partner announced that pursuant to the Partnership Agreement of the above named Limited Partnership, a special meeting of the Partners was held on the _____ day of _____, 20____ at _____ o'clock ___M. The chairman then declared that the meeting was to be held in compliance with applicable statutes.

The chairman of the meeting then discussed granting full signatory authority to _____ sign any and all banking documents or instruments, contracts and/or any other documents as needed on behalf of this Partnership.

The chairman of the meeting then requested that the Partners confer upon the above named individual full signatory authority to represent the interests of this Partnership in signing all banking documents or instruments negotiating and executing contract(s) and or any and all other documents relating to this Partnership.

On motion duly made and carried, it was, **RESOLVED** and **ORDERED** that the person named above, is henceforth granted the full signatory authority and power to enter into any and all agreements as necessary, and to negotiate and execute contract(s) or any other necessary documents relating to this Partnership.

There being no further business requiring Partner action or consideration on a motion duly made, seconded and carried, the meeting was adjourned.

CERTIFICATION OF PARTNERSHIP GENERAL PARTNER

I the undersigned, certify that I am the duly appointed General Partner of the above named Partnership and that the forgoing Resolution is a true and accurate copy of a Resolution duly adopted at a meeting of the Partners thereof, convened and held in accordance with the Partnership Agreement of said Partnership and that the Resolution is now in full force and effect.

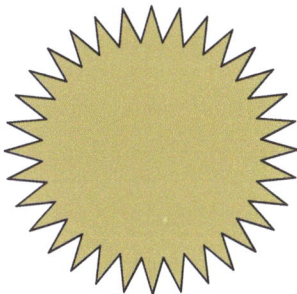

IN WITNESS THEREOF, I have affixed my name as General Partner of the above named Partnership and have attached the seal of said Partnership to this Resolution.

Dated _____ 20____

_____
Partnership General Partner

MINUTES OF A SPECIAL MEETING OF THE PARTNERS OF
(Replace This With The Name Of Your LP)
A (Name of State) LIMITED PARTNERSHIP
FOR
USE OF PERSONAL CREDIT CARD

The General Partner announced that pursuant to the Partnership Agreement of the above named Limited Partnership, a special meeting of the Partners was held on the _____ day of _____, 20____ at _____ o'clock ___M. The chairman then declared that the meeting was to be held in compliance with applicable statutes.

The chairman of the meeting then discussed having one or more of the Partners of the above named Partnership use their personal credit and/or credit cards to facilitate the needs of the Partnership due to the fact that the Partnership while earning money, has no credit history (credit worthiness) and the Partner(s) in question have credit worthiness but lack financial resources.

On motion duly made and carried, it was **RESOLVED** and **ORDERED** that the following individuals would be authorized to state the Partnership's income on any application for credit (intended for the use of the Partnership only) in conjunction with said Partner's personal credit history in order to secure credit and or credit cards to be primarily used for the benefit of this Partnership. In addition, it was **RESOLVED** and **ORDERED** that this Partnership shall directly pay (by check) all charges associated with the issuance of said credit/cards and/or the payment for any purchases using said credit/cards by this Partnership.

_____   _____
Printed Name   Signature

CERTIFICATION OF PARTNERSHIP GENERAL PARTNER

I the undersigned, certify that I am the duly appointed General Partner of the above named Partnership and that the forgoing Resolution is a true and accurate copy of a Resolution duly adopted at a meeting of the Partners thereof, convened and held in accordance with the Partnership Agreement of said Partnership and that the Resolution is now in full force and effect.

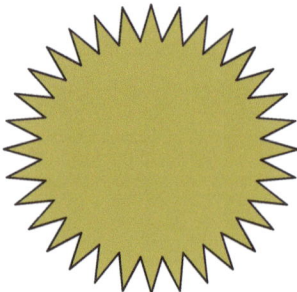

IN WITNESS THEREOF, I have affixed my name as General Partner of the above named Partnership and have attached the seal of said Partnership to this Resolution.

Dated _____ 20____

_____
Partnership General Partner

MINUTES OF A SPECIAL MEETING OF PARTNERS OF
(Replace This With The Name Of Your LP)
A (Name of State) LIMITED PARTNERSHIP
FOR
TERMINATION AND REPLACEMENT
OF GENERAL PARTNER

The General Partner announced that pursuant to the Partnership Agreement of the above named Limited Partnership, a special meeting of the Partners was held on the _____ day of _____, 20___ at _____ o'clock __M. The chairman then declared that the meeting was to be held in compliance with applicable statutes.

The chairman of the meeting declared that the meeting was to be held in compliance with applicable statutes, for the purpose of terminating the current General Partner and to appoint a new General Partner for the above named Partnership.

After a brief discussion and the unanimous agreement of the partners, the chairman of the meeting stated that it was **RESOLVED** by unanimous agreement, that the termination of _____ as the General Partner and the appointment of _____ as the new General Partner for the above named Partnership is approved by the partnership as of the date first written above. Additionally, it was **RESOLVED** and agreed by the partners that this new appointment shall become effective as of the date first written above.

There being no further business requiring partner action or consideration, on a motion duly made, seconded and carried, the meeting was adjourned.

CERTIFICATION OF PARTNERSHIP GENERAL PARTNER

I the undersigned, certify that I am the duly appointed General Partner of the above named Partnership and that the forgoing Resolution is a true and accurate copy of a Resolution duly adopted at a meeting of the Partners thereof, convened and held in accordance with the Partnership Agreement of said Partnership and that the Resolution is now in full force and effect.

IN WITNESS THEREOF, I have affixed my name as General Partner of the above named Partnership and have attached the seal of said Partnership to this Resolution.

Dated _____ 20___

_____
Partnership General Partner

**Business Preservation Trust
Documents**

AssetProtectionServices.com

Addendum to Trust Agreement dated this _____ day of_____, 20___.

WHEREAS, a certain Trust Agreement (hereinafter "Trust Agreement") was duly executed on the _____ day of _____, 20___ by and between _____, as Grantor(s) and _____, as Trustee of the trust created thereby known as the _____ Trust (hereinafter referred to as the "Trust") for the purposes of said trustee to hold the real and/or personal property for the purposes stated in the Trust Agreement, and

WHEREAS, the current beneficiaries, _____ whose interests represent the entire beneficial interest under the Trust are desirous of modifying the terms of said Business Preservation Trust Agreement, and

WHEREAS, the current Trustee is, _____ ("trustee of record") is also agreeable to modifying the terms of said Business Preservation Trust Agreement, the parties agree as follows:

1. A co-trustee, _____, whose address is_____, will be added as co-trustee to serve with the above-named trustee. Said co-trustee will have the same rights, powers and duties as the Trustee of Record under the above-referenced trust agreement, and may act independently without the signature of the Trustee of Record as stated in the trust agreement, a copy of which is annexed and incorporated by reference.

2. All actions taken by the trustees shall be with the consent of the other, though such consent need not be in writing. In the case of any disagreement between the trustees, such controversy shall be submitted to the beneficiaries, who, by majority vote, will make a decision which shall be binding on the trustees.

OPTIONAL PARAGRAPH IF THE TRUST HOLDS REAL ESTATE

3. The co-trustee, in additional to the powers set forth in the trust agreement, shall have the power, authority and discretion (unless otherwise directed by the beneficiaries), to manage the trust property, including the power to rent, lease, option, mortgage, sell, hypothecate said property and the powers of maintaining bank accounts in the name of the trust, collecting rents, advertising for vacancies, maintaining the premises, grounds, common areas, electrical, heating, plumbing and other utilities, paying taxes and other assessments when due, holding security deposits in escrow for tenants, executing leases, painting, fixing and repairing the interior of rental units; taking possession of the premises when vacant, paying the mortgages, insurance and homeowners' association dues from net monthly rents and taking any steps necessary in his or her discretion to maintain the value of the property.

ADDENDUM TO TRUST AGREEMENT

IN WITNESS WHEREOF, the parties hereto have executed this agreement as of the day and year first above written.

_____   _____

Beneficiary   Beneficiary

ACKNOWLEDGED BY CO-TRUSTEE

_____

Co-Trustee

NOTARY ACKNOWLEDGEMENT

STATE OF _____)

) SS.

COUNTY OF _____)

On _____ before me, _____

(insert name and title of the officer)

personally appeared _____, who proved to me on the basis of satisfactory evidence to be the person(s) whose name(s) is are subscribed to the within instrument and acknowledged to me that he/she/they executed the same in his/her/their authorized capacity(ies), and that by his/her/their signature(s) on the instrument the person(s), or the entity upon behalf of which the person(s) acted, executed the instrument.

I certify under PENALTY OF PERJURY under the laws of the State of _____ that the foregoing paragraph is true and correct.

WITNESS my hand and official seal.

_____

Notary Public Signature

ADDENDUM TO TRUST AGREEMENT

ACKNOWLEDGED BY TRUSTEE OF RECORD

_____
Trustee of Record

NOTARY ACKNOWLEDGEMENT

STATE OF _____)

) SS.

COUNTY OF _____)

On _____ before me, _____

(insert name and title of the officer)

personally appeared _____, who proved to me on the basis of satisfactory evidence to be the person(s) whose name(s) is are subscribed to the within instrument and acknowledged to me that he/she/they executed the same in his/her/their authorized capacity(ies), and that by his/her/their signature(s) on the instrument the person(s), or the entity upon behalf of which the person(s) acted, executed the instrument.

I certify under PENALTY OF PERJURY under the laws of the State of _____ that the foregoing paragraph is true and correct.

WITNESS my hand and official seal.

_____
Notary Public Signature

AFFIDAVIT OF RESIGNATION OF TRUSTEE
AND
APPOINTMENT OF SUCCESSOR TRUSTEE

1. This affidavit is made relating to trust property held in a trust in the State of _____.

2. The legal description of the trust property is stated on the attached Exhibit "A".

3. The name of the trust is _____.

4. The trustee of record for this trust is _____, whose address is _____. The duties of said trustee shall expire on _____/_____, 20___.

5. The successor trustee is _____, whose address is _____. _____. Said successor trustee shall commence his/her/its duties on _____/_____, 20___ with the same rights, powers and duties of his/her/its predecessor trustee.

_____
Resigning Trustee

NOTARY ACKNOWLEDGEMENT

STATE OF _____)
) SS.
COUNTY OF _____)

On _____ before me, _____
                                                (insert name and title of the officer)

personally appeared _____, who proved to me on the basis of satisfactory evidence to be the person(s) whose name(s) is are subscribed to the within instrument and acknowledged to me that he/she/they executed the same in his/her/their authorized capacity(ies), and that by his/her/their signature(s) on the instrument the person(s), or the entity upon behalf of which the person(s) acted, executed the instrument.

I certify under PENALTY OF PERJURY under the laws of the State of _____ that the foregoing paragraph is true and correct.

                                  WITNESS my hand and official seal.

_____
Notary Public Signature

ACKNOWLEDGMENT FOR SUCCESSOR TRUSTEE

_____
Successor Trustee

NOTARY ACKNOWLEDGEMENT

STATE OF _____)
) SS.
COUNTY OF _____)

On _____ before me, _____
                                                    (insert name and title of the officer)

personally appeared _____, who proved to me on the basis of satisfactory evidence to be the person(s) whose name(s) is are subscribed to the within instrument and acknowledged to me that he/she/they executed the same in his/her/their authorized capacity(ies), and that by his/her/their signature(s) on the instrument the person(s), or the entity upon behalf of which the person(s) acted, executed the instrument.

I certify under PENALTY OF PERJURY under the laws of the State of _____ that the foregoing paragraph is true and correct.

WITNESS my hand and official seal.

_____
Notary Public Signature

ASSIGNMENT
OF
BENEFICIAL INTEREST IN TRUST

The undersigned ("Assignor"), for $_____ received in hand and for other valuable consideration, hereby assigns all right, title and interest in the beneficial interest, including the power of direction and revocation, under a certain Trust Agreement created the _____ day of _____, 20___ by and between _____ _____ as grantor(s) and _____ as Trustee(s) known as the "_____Business Preservation Trust", which owns certain business property shown on the attached Exhibit "A" to _____ ("Assignee") whose address is _____.

I/We hereby affirm and warrant that the beneficial interest assigned herein is _____% of the total beneficial interest in the aforesaid Trust, and that I/We have the full power and authority to assign and transfer said interest. I/We further agree to waive any right to revoke or amend said trust or in any way to direct, influence or control the actions of the trustee(s) which would create an ownership interest as defined in Section 671-678 of the Internal Revenue Code.

We intend this transfer to be a transfer of personal property for federal income tax purposes, and we agree to report the same to the Internal Revenue Service if required to do so by law.

_____   _____
Assignor   Assignor

ASSIGNMENT
OF
BENEFICIAL INTEREST IN TRUST

NOTARY ACKNOWLEDGEMENT

STATE OF _____)
) SS.

COUNTY OF _____)

On _____ before me, _____

(insert name and title of the officer)

personally appeared _____, who proved to me on the basis of satisfactory evidence to be the person(s) whose name(s) is are subscribed to the within instrument and acknowledged to me that he/she/they executed the same in his/her/their authorized capacity(ies), and that by his/her/their signature(s) on the instrument the person(s), or the entity upon behalf of which the person(s) acted, executed the instrument.

I certify under PENALTY OF PERJURY under the laws of the State of _____ that the foregoing paragraph is true and correct.

WITNESS my hand and official seal.

_____
Notary Public Signature

ACKNOWLEDGMENT FOR ASSIGNEE(S)

I/we accept the foregoing assignment of beneficial interest subject to all of the terms and conditions of the trust agreement and any addendums thereto.

_____   _____
Assignee   Assignee

ACKNOWLEDGMENT OF TRUSTEE

I have received a copy of this Assignment of beneficial interest and acknowledge the validity of said assignment subject to all of the terms and conditions of the trust agreement and any addendums thereto.

_____
Trustee

DECLARATION
OF
BENEFICIAL INTEREST
IN
(*REPLACE WITH TRUST NAME*)

I/we, the undersigned as the holder(s) of the beneficial Interest (ownership) in the above named trust, hereby declare and say that;

1. All of the beneficial interest in the trust and its assets as well as all rights, powers, privileges in said trust are held by the undersigned entity and/or individual **only**; and,

2. The undersigned states that he/she/it fully understands his/her/its legal rights and obligations in connection herewith and that having understood the rights and obligations detailed herein, has executed this instrument on this the _____ Day of _____ 20___.

BENEFICIARY NAME: *(PUT IN COMPANY OR PERSONAL NAME)*
SIGNATURE: _____

BENEFICIARY NAME: *(PUT IN COMPANY OR PERSONAL NAME)*
SIGNATURE: _____

NOTARY ACKNOWLEDGEMENT

STATE OF _____)
) SS.
COUNTY OF _____)

On _____ before me, _____
(insert name and title of the officer)

personally appeared _____, who proved to me on the basis of satisfactory evidence to be the person(s) whose name(s) is are subscribed to the within instrument and acknowledged to me that he/she/they executed the same in his/her/their authorized capacity(ies), and that by his/her/their signature(s) on the instrument the person(s), or the entity upon behalf of which the person(s) acted, executed the instrument.

I certify under PENALTY OF PERJURY under the laws of the State of _____ that the foregoing paragraph is true and correct.

WITNESS my hand and official seal.

_____
Notary Public Signature

The endorsement made below by _____, the Trustee of _____ trust is made with the express understanding that the Trustee is signing on behalf of said trust and not personally, in the exercise of the power and authority vested by said trust and the Trustee shall bear no personal liability whatsoever for the obligations incurred by his or her signature. Nothing contained in herein shall create any personal liability, culpability or guarantee on the part of the Trustee, his or her heirs or assigns.

EXTENSION OF TRUST AGREEMENT

Addendum to Trust Agreement dated this _____ day of _____, 20___.

WHEREAS, a Trust Agreement (hereinafter "Trust Agreement") was duly executed on the _____ day of _____, 20___ by and between _____ _____, as Grantor(s)/Settlor(s) and _____, as Trustee of Record for the trust created thereby known as the _____, (hereinafter referred to as the "Trust") for the purposes of said trustee to hold real and/or personal property for the purposes stated in the Trust Agreement, and

WHEREAS, the beneficiaries, _____, whose interests represent the entire beneficial interest under the Trust are desirous of extending the term of said Trust Agreement, and

WHEREAS, the Trustee,_____, is also agreeable to extending the term of said Trust Agreement, the parties agree as follows:
The term of said trust agreement shall be extended to _____/_____ 20___.

IN WITNESS WHEREOF, the parties hereto have executed this agreement as of the day and year first above written.

_____
Beneficiary

NOTARY ACKNOWLEDGEMENT

STATE OF _____)
) SS.
COUNTY OF _____)

On _____ before me, _____
(insert name and title of the officer)
personally appeared _____, who proved to me on the basis of satisfactory evidence to be the person(s) whose name(s) is are subscribed to the within instrument and acknowledged to me that he/she/they executed the same in his/her/ their authorized capacity(ies), and that by his/her/their signature(s) on the instrument the person(s), or the entity upon behalf of which the person(s) acted, executed the instrument.

I certify under PENALTY OF PERJURY under the laws of the State of _____ that the foregoing paragraph is true and correct.

WITNESS my hand and official seal.

_____
Notary Public Signature

EXTENSION OF TRUST AGREEMENT

_____
Trustee

NOTARY ACKNOWLEDGEMENT

STATE OF _____)
) SS.
COUNTY OF _____)

On _____ before me, _____
(insert name and title of the officer)

personally appeared _____, who proved to me on the basis of satisfactory evidence to be the person(s) whose name(s) is are subscribed to the within instrument and acknowledged to me that he/she/they executed the same in his/her/their authorized capacity(ies), and that by his/her/their signature(s) on the instrument the person(s), or the entity upon behalf of which the person(s) acted, executed the instrument.

I certify under PENALTY OF PERJURY under the laws of the State of _____ that the foregoing paragraph is true and correct.

WITNESS my hand and official seal.

_____
Notary Public Signature

--------------------[SPACE ABOVE RESERVED FOR RECORDING IF REQUIRED]-----------------

RESIGNATION OF CO-TRUSTEE

To the beneficiary(ies) of record for _____ trust.

1. This Resignation of the Co-Trustee of _____ trust.

2. The resigning co-trustee is _____, whose status as said co-trustee expired on ____/_____/20___.

3. Said resignation shall become effective from the _____ day of _____ 20___.

_____
Resigning co-Trustee

The undersigned, as Grantor(s) of the above named trust, does/do hereby revoke said trust effective this date.

NOTICE: A copy of this revocation has been mailed to the below-named trustee of record. And a further copy of this revocation has been mailed to the below-named beneficiary (ies):

_____   _____

RECORDING: A signed original of this notice of revocation may or has been duly recorded with the county recorder's office in the following counties if property has been placed in the name of the trust named herein:

_____   _____

PROPERTY TRANSFERS: Should any property be "titled" in the name of the trust named herein, said property shall be transferred to the following, prior to this trust being revoked (terminated):

Name: _____

Address:_____

_____

This revocation made under oath and the stated facts herein affirmed as true and correct this the _____ Day of _____ 20___,

_____   _____
Grantor Printed Name   Grantor Signature

_____   _____
Witness Printed Name   Witness Signature

Address: _____   _____

_____   _____
Witness Printed Name   Witness Signature

Address: _____   _____

TRUSTEE NOTICE OF RESIGNATION

TO: _____, Beneficiaries of the

_____Trust.

Please be advised that I desire to resign my office as trustee of the above-mentioned Trust effective _____, 20___.

Under the terms of our Trust Agreement, you have sixty-(60) days to appoint a successor trustee. Upon notification of the name and address of the successor trustee, I will execute all documents necessary for the transfer of the office of trustee.

In the event that I do not receive a notice of successor trustee by _____, 20___, I will transfer the title(s) to the Trust Property (if any) to you pursuant to your interests as stated in the trust agreement.

Dated: _____/_____ 20___

_____
Trustee

TRUSTEE NOTICE OF TERMINATION

TO: _____, Trustee.

Please be advised that I/we desire to terminate your office as trustee of the
_____ Trust

effective _____, 20___.

The new trustee's name is _____, and whose

address is _____

_____.

Please turn over all books, records, funds and bank statements to said new trustee (if any).

Please execute the enclosed affidavit and return the originals to the undersigned.

Dated: _____/_____ 20___

_____
Beneficiary

_____
Beneficiary

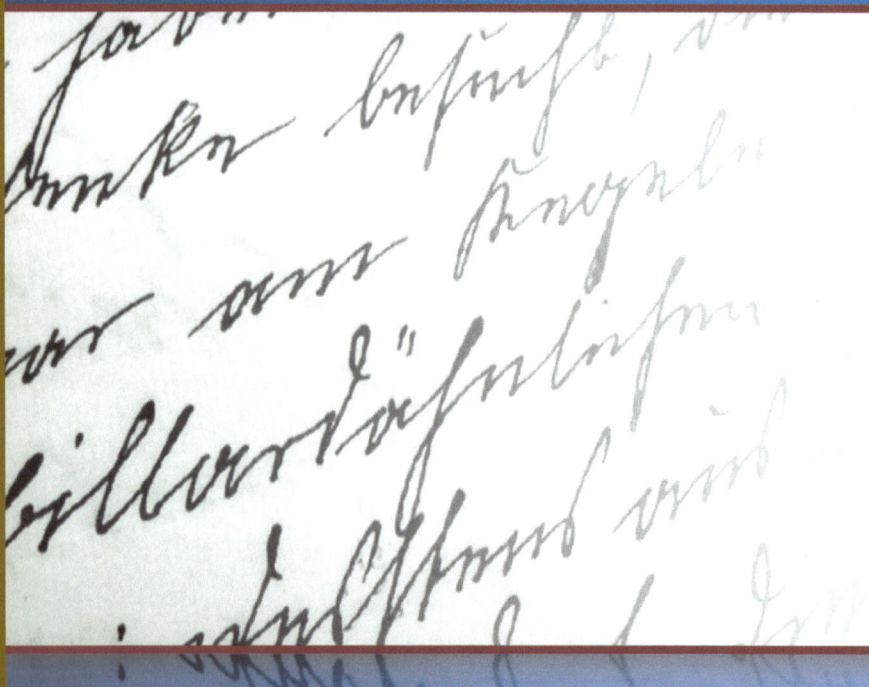

Revocable Living Trust
Documents

Family and Friends

Brother _____ Relationship _____

Mailing Address _____

City _____ State _____ Zip _____ Country_____

Home +____ (_____) _____ - _____   Work +____ (_____) _____ - _____

Mobile +____ (_____) _____ - _____   Fax +____ (_____) _____ - _____

Skype _____   Other _____

E-Mail_____

Notes _____

_____

_____

Sister _____ Relationship _____

Mailing Address _____

City _____ State _____ Zip _____ Country_____

Home +____ (_____) _____ - _____   Work +____ (_____) _____ - _____

Mobile +____ (_____) _____ - _____   Fax +____ (_____) _____ - _____

Skype _____   Other _____

E-Mail_____

Notes _____

_____

_____

Declaration of Final Arrangements

Family and Friends

Friend _____ Relationship _____

Mailing Address _____

City _____ State _____ Zip _____ Country_____

Home +____ (_____) _____ - _____   Work +____ (_____) _____ - _____

Mobile +____ (_____) _____ - _____   Fax +____ (_____) _____ - _____

Skype _____   Other _____

E-Mail_____

Notes _____

_____

_____

_____

Other _____ Relationship _____

Mailing Address _____

City _____ State _____ Zip _____ Country_____

Home +____ (_____) _____ - _____   Work +____ (_____) _____ - _____

Mobile +____ (_____) _____ - _____   Fax +____ (_____) _____ - _____

Skype _____   Other _____

E-Mail_____

Notes _____

_____

_____

Primary Advisors

Accountant _____ Assistant _____

Company _____

Mailing Address _____

City _____ State _____ Zip _____ Country_____

Work +____ (_____) _____ - _____   Fax +____ (_____) _____ - _____

Mobile +____ (_____) _____ - _____   Skype_____

E-Mail _____

Website _____

Notes _____

_____

Attorney _____ Assistant _____

Company _____

Mailing Address _____

City _____ State _____ Zip _____ Country_____

Work +____ (_____) _____ - _____   Fax +____ (_____) _____ - _____

Mobile +____ (_____) _____ - _____   Skype_____

E-Mail _____

Website _____

Notes _____

_____

Declaration of Final Arrangements

Primary Advisors

Banker _____ Assistant _____

Company _____

Mailing Address _____

City _____ State _____ Zip _____ Country_____

Work +____ (_____) _____ - _____   Fax +____ (_____) _____ - _____

Mobile +____ (_____) _____ - _____   Skype_____

E-Mail _____

Website _____

Notes _____

_____

Doctor _____ Assistant _____

Company _____

Mailing Address _____

City _____ State _____ Zip _____ Country_____

Work +____ (_____) _____ - _____   Fax +____ (_____) _____ - _____

Mobile +____ (_____) _____ - _____   Skype_____

E-Mail _____

Website _____

Notes _____

_____

Declaration of Final Arrangements

Primary Advisors

Employer _____ Assistant _____

Company _____

Mailing Address _____

City _____ State _____ Zip _____ Country_____

Work +_____ (_____) _____ - _____   Fax +_____ (_____) _____ - _____

Mobile +_____ (_____) _____ - _____   Skype_____

E-Mail _____

Website _____

Notes _____

_____

Funeral Home _____ Assistant _____

Company _____

Mailing Address _____

City _____ State _____ Zip _____ Country_____

Work +_____ (_____) _____ - _____   Fax +_____ (_____) _____ - _____

Mobile +_____ (_____) _____ - _____   Skype_____

E-Mail _____

Website _____

Notes _____

_____

Declaration of Final Arrangements

Primary Advisors

Insurance Agent _____ Assistant _____

Company _____

Mailing Address _____

City _____ State _____ Zip _____ Country_____

Work +____ (_____) _____ - _____   Fax +____ (_____) _____ - _____

Mobile +____ (_____) _____ - _____   Skype_____

E-Mail _____

Website _____

Notes _____

_____

Investment Advisor _____ Assistant _____

Company _____

Mailing Address _____

City _____ State _____ Zip _____ Country_____

Work +____ (_____) _____ - _____   Fax +____ (_____) _____ - _____

Mobile +____ (_____) _____ - _____   Skype_____

E-Mail _____

Website _____

Notes _____

_____

Declaration of Final Arrangements

Primary Advisors

Religious Leader _____ Assistant _____

Company _____

Mailing Address _____

City _____ State _____ Zip _____ Country_____

Work +____ (_____) _____ - _____   Fax +____ (_____) _____ - _____

Mobile +____ (_____) _____ - _____   Skype_____

E-Mail _____

Website _____

Notes _____

_____

Other _____ Assistant _____

Company _____

Mailing Address _____

City _____ State _____ Zip _____ Country_____

Work +____ (_____) _____ - _____   Fax +____ (_____) _____ - _____

Mobile +____ (_____) _____ - _____   Skype_____

E-Mail _____

Website _____

Notes _____

_____

Document Locator

Banking Records	Bank Statements	Location _____
	Check Books	Location _____
	Certificates of Deposit	Location _____
	Credit Card Records	Location _____
	Safe Deposit Boxes	Location _____
Company Documents	Corporations	Location _____
	Contractor Agreements	Location _____
	Employment Records	Location _____
	Foundations	Location _____
	Limited Liability Companies	Location _____
	Limited Partnerships	Location _____
	Revocable / Irrevocable Trusts	Location _____
Digital Records	Computer	Password _____
	Blogs / Newsletters / Photos	Password _____
	Facebook / Twitter / Skype	Password _____
	Domain Name Registrations	Password _____
	E-Mail Accounts	Password _____
	Software Registrations	Password _____
Insurance Policies	Car Insurance Policies	Location _____
	Health Insurance Policies	Location _____
	Home Insurance Policies	Location _____
	Life Insurance Policies	Location _____
	Rental Insurance Policies	Location _____
	Title Insurance Policies	Location _____
Investment Accounts	Annuity Contracts	Location _____
	Brokerage Account Records	Location _____
	Stock and Bond Certificates	Location _____
	401-K Account Records	Location _____
	Individual Retirement Accounts	Location _____
	Self-Employment Plans (SEP)	Location _____
Legal Paperwork	Birth Certificate	Location _____
	Citizenship Paperwork	Location _____
	Divorce Records	Location _____
	Marriage Licenses	Location _____
	Military Records	Location _____

Declaration of Final Arrangements

Document Locator

Personal Property

Airplane Titles	Location _____
Automobile Titles	Location _____
Boat Titles	Location _____
Jewelry / Artwork Registrations	Location _____

Real Estate Titles

Loan Contracts and Notes	Location _____
Real Estate Deeds	Location _____
Rental Property Records	Location _____

Tax Records

Federal Tax Returns	Location _____
Gift Tax Returns	Location _____
International Tax Returns	Location _____
State Tax Returns	Location _____

Personal Effects

_____	Location _____
_____	Location _____
_____	Location _____
_____	Location _____
_____	Location _____

Other

_____	Location _____
_____	Location _____
_____	Location _____
_____	Location _____
_____	Location _____

_____	_____	_____ _____
	_____	_____ _____
	_____	_____ _____
	_____	_____ _____
	_____	_____ _____

_____	_____	_____ _____
	_____	_____ _____
	_____	_____ _____
	_____	_____ _____
	_____	_____ _____

Declaration of Final Arrangements

Funeral Services

Notification

   I desire that my "Religious Leader" be contacted to offer assistance and comfort to survivors.

Funeral Home

   I desire that my "Funeral Home" be contacted to make the arrangements requested herein.

Treatment of Body

   I desire that my body be _____.

Pre-Funeral Services *(Often Private)*

   • I desire for anyone wishing to attend _____ be welcome or _____ not be welcome.
   • The location shall be at _____.
   • My body _____ may be present / _____ may not be present.
   • The following music to be played. *(Attached CD or USB Jump Drive)*
   • The following text is to be read aloud. *(Attached Selections of Scripture or Text)*
   • The following biographical information is to be displayed. *(Attached Photos and Bio)*
   • The following people are to speak _____.
   • Floral arrangements are to be provided by_____.

Memorial Services *(Often Public)*

   • I desire for anyone wishing to attend _____ be welcome or _____ not be welcome.
   • The location shall be at _____.
   • My body _____ may be present / _____ may not be present.
   • The following music to be played. *(Attached CD or USB Jump Drive)*
   • The following text is to be read aloud. *(Attached Selections of Scripture or Text)*
   • The following biographical information is to be displayed. *(Attached Photos and Bio)*
   • The following people are to speak _____.
   • Floral arrangements are to be provided by_____.

Funeral Services *(Often Public)*

   • I desire for anyone wishing to attend _____ be welcome or _____ not be welcome.
   • The location shall be at _____.
   • My body _____ may be present / _____ may not be present.
   • The following music to be played. *(Attached CD or USB Jump Drive)*
   • The following text is to be read aloud. *(Attached Selections of Scripture or Text)*
   • The following biographical information is to be displayed. *(Attached Photos and Bio)*
   • The following people are to speak _____.
   • Floral arrangements are to be provided by_____.

Post-Funeral Services *(Often Private)*

- I desire for anyone wishing to attend _____ be welcome or _____ not be welcome.
- The location shall be at _____.
- My body _____ may be present / _____ may not be present.
- The following music to be played. *(Attached CD or USB Jump Drive)*
- The following text is to be read aloud. *(Attached Selections of Scripture or Text)*
- The following biographical information is to be displayed. *(Attached Photos and Bio)*
- The following people are to speak _____.
- Floral arrangements are to be provided by_____.

Obituary

An obituary notice shall be published in _____.

Additional Wishes

_____

_____

_____

_____

_____

_____

Declaration of Final Arrangements

Having given careful thought and consideration to these instructions, I hope that my desires will be fulfilled to the best extent possible. I understand this Declaration is not legally binding and that the ultimate responsibility and decision to honor my desires shall be made by my survivors based on the circumstances at the time of my death.

Executed this _____ day of _____, 20___

_____
(Your) Signature

AFFIDAVIT OF SUCCESSION
TO
_____ **LIVING TRUST**

BE IT KNOWN that the undersigned Successor Trustee, under the
_____ Living Trust, hereby assumes the duties of Successor Trustee
as specified in said trust and that Settlor, *(Settlor)*, is now incapacitated or deceased.

WHEREFORE, the Successor Trustee has assumed title to the real property and other assets
covered by the _____ Living Trust and will hereafter administer the
same in accordance with the instructions set forth in said trust.

_____
Successor Trustee

NOTARY ACKNOWLEDGEMENT

STATE OF _____)
) SS.
COUNTY OF _____)

On _____ before me, _____
                                            (insert name and title of the officer)

personally appeared _____, who proved to
me on the basis of satisfactory evidence to be the person(s) whose name(s) is are subscribed to
the within instrument and acknowledged to me that he/she/they executed the same in his/her/
their authorized capacity(ies), and that by his/her/their signature(s) on the instrument the
person(s), or the entity upon behalf of which the person(s) acted, executed the instrument.

I certify under PENALTY OF PERJURY under the laws of the State of _____
that the foregoing paragraph is true and correct.

WITNESS my hand and official seal.

_____
Notary Public Signature

AMENDMENT
TO
_____ **LIVING TRUST**

The _____ Living Trust, by and between *(Settlor)* and *(Trustee)*, shall be amended by substituting, adding or deleting the following provisions:

_____

_____

_____

_____

_____

_____

_____

All provisions of the _____ Living Trust are hereby incorporated by reference herein with the exception of the provisions expressly modified by this amendment.

_____
Settlor

NOTARY ACKNOWLEDGEMENT

STATE OF _____)

) SS.

COUNTY OF _____)

On _____ before me, _____
(insert name and title of the officer)

personally appeared _____, who proved to me on the basis of satisfactory evidence to be the person(s) whose name(s) is are subscribed to the within instrument and acknowledged to me that he/she/they executed the same in his/her/their authorized capacity(ies), and that by his/her/their signature(s) on the instrument the person(s), or the entity upon behalf of which the person(s) acted, executed the instrument.

I certify under PENALTY OF PERJURY under the laws of the State of _____ that the foregoing paragraph is true and correct.

WITNESS my hand and official seal.

_____
Notary Public Signature

AMENDMENT
TO
_____ LIVING TRUST

_____
Trustee

NOTARY ACKNOWLEDGEMENT

STATE OF _____)
) SS.

COUNTY OF _____)

On _____ before me, _____

(insert name and title of the officer)

personally appeared _____, who proved to me on the basis of satisfactory evidence to be the person(s) whose name(s) is are subscribed to the within instrument and acknowledged to me that he/she/they executed the same in his/her/their authorized capacity(ies), and that by his/her/their signature(s) on the instrument the person(s), or the entity upon behalf of which the person(s) acted, executed the instrument.

I certify under PENALTY OF PERJURY under the laws of the State of _____ that the foregoing paragraph is true and correct.

WITNESS my hand and official seal.

_____
Notary Public Signature

ASSIGNMENT OF PROPERTY
TO
_____ LIVING TRUST

Settlor, does hereby sell, transfer and convey unto the Trustee of the
_____ Living Trust, the following property:

_____

_____

_____

_____

_____

_____

_____

To have and to hold for the benefit of the _____ Living Trust, its
beneficiaries, successors and assigns. Seller warrants to defend the sale of property against all
and every person claiming an adverse interest to the same.

_____

Settlor

NOTARY ACKNOWLEDGEMENT

STATE OF _____)

) SS.

COUNTY OF _____)

On _____ before me, _____

(insert name and title of the officer)

personally appeared _____, who proved to
me on the basis of satisfactory evidence to be the person(s) whose name(s) is are subscribed to
the within instrument and acknowledged to me that he/she/they executed the same in his/her/
their authorized capacity(ies), and that by his/her/their signature(s) on the instrument the
person(s), or the entity upon behalf of which the person(s) acted, executed the instrument.

I certify under PENALTY OF PERJURY under the laws of the State of _____
that the foregoing paragraph is true and correct.

WITNESS my hand and official seal.

_____

Notary Public Signature

BILL OF SALE
TO
_____ **LIVING TRUST**

BE IT KNOWN, for good consideration, and in the payment amount of $ _____ ,
(written amount) _____ dollars, the receipt and sufficiency
of which is acknowledged, the undersigned Seller _____
whose mailing address is: _____
City_____ State_____ Zip_____ Country_____ ,
hereby sells and transfers to the Buyer _____ whose
mailing address is: _____
City_____ State_____ Zip_____ Country_____ ,
and the Buyer's successors and assigns forever, the following described chattels and personal
property: _____

The Seller warrants to Buyer it has good and marketable title to said property, full authority to
sell and transfer said property, and that said property is sold free of all liens, encumbrances,
liabilities and adverse claims of every nature and description whatsoever.

Seller further warrants to Buyer that it will fully defend, protect, indemnify and hold harmless the
Buyer and its lawful successors and assigns from any adverse claim made hereto by all persons
whomsoever. Said property is sold in "as is" condition and where presently located.

_____
Seller

NOTARY ACKNOWLEDGEMENT

STATE OF _____)
COUNTY OF _____)
On _____ before me, _____
(insert name and title of the officer)
personally appeared _____, who proved to
me on the basis of satisfactory evidence to be the person(s) whose name(s) is are subscribed to
the within instrument and acknowledged to me that he/she/they executed the same in his/her/
their authorized capacity(ies), and that by his/her/their signature(s) on the instrument the
person(s), or the entity upon behalf of which the person(s) acted, executed the instrument.

I certify under PENALTY OF PERJURY under the laws of the State of _____
that the foregoing paragraph is true and correct.

WITNESS my hand and official seal.

_____
Notary Public Signature

QUITCLAIM DEED
TO
_____ **LIVING TRUST**

THIS QUITCLAIM DEED, executed this day by:

The First Party, _____, whose mailing address is

_____

City_____ State_____ Zip_____ Country_____ ,
to the Second Party: _____, whose mailing address is

_____

City_____ State_____ Zip_____ Country_____ ,

WITNESSETH, that the said First Party, for good consideration and for the sum of
$ _____ (USD) or *(written amount)* _____ dollars,
paid by the said Second Party, the receipt whereof is hereby acknowledged, does hereby
remise, release and quitclaim unto the said Second Party forever, all the right title, interest and
claim which the said First Party has in and to the following described property, parcel of land,
and improvements and appurtenances thereto in the County of _____, State
of _____.

_____
First Party

NOTARY ACKNOWLEDGEMENT

STATE OF _____)
) SS.
COUNTY OF _____)

On _____ before me, _____
                                       (insert name and title of the officer)

personally appeared _____, who proved to
me on the basis of satisfactory evidence to be the person(s) whose name(s) is are subscribed to
the within instrument and acknowledged to me that he/she/they executed the same in his/her/
their authorized capacity(ies), and that by his/her/their signature(s) on the instrument the
person(s), or the entity upon behalf of which the person(s) acted, executed the instrument.

I certify under PENALTY OF PERJURY under the laws of the State of _____
that the foregoing paragraph is true and correct.

WITNESS my hand and official seal.

_____
Notary Public Signature

QUITCLAIM DEED
TO
_____ **LIVING TRUST**

_____
Second Party

NOTARY ACKNOWLEDGEMENT

STATE OF _____)
) SS.
COUNTY OF _____)

On _____ before me, _____
                                                      (insert name and title of the officer)

personally appeared _____, who proved to
me on the basis of satisfactory evidence to be the person(s) whose name(s) is are subscribed to
the within instrument and acknowledged to me that he/she/they executed the same in his/her/
their authorized capacity(ies), and that by his/her/their signature(s) on the instrument the
person(s), or the entity upon behalf of which the person(s) acted, executed the instrument.

I certify under PENALTY OF PERJURY under the laws of the State of _____
that the foregoing paragraph is true and correct.

                                         WITNESS my hand and official seal.

                                         _____
                                         Notary Public Signature

The undersigned Settlor, of the _____ Living Trust, does hereby revoke said trust effective this date.

NOTICE: A copy of this Revocation of Trust of _____ Living Trust has been mailed to the following trustees and beneficiaries:

Trustee _____   **Trustee** _____

Address _____   Address _____

    City _____   City _____

    State _____ Zip _____   State _____ Zip _____

    Country _____   Country _____

Beneficiary _____   **Beneficiary** _____

Address _____   Address _____

    City _____   City _____

    State _____ Zip _____   State _____ Zip _____

    Country _____   Country _____

RECORDING: A signed original copy of this Revocation of Trust of _____ Living Trust has been duly recorded with the county recorder's office in the following counties:

County _____   **County** _____

Address _____   Address _____

    City _____   City _____

    State _____ Zip _____   State _____ Zip _____

REVOCATION
OF
_____ **LIVING TRUST**

_____
Settlor

NOTARY ACKNOWLEDGEMENT

STATE OF _____)
) SS.
COUNTY OF _____)

On _____ before me, _____
(insert name and title of the officer)

personally appeared _____, who proved to me on the basis of satisfactory evidence to be the person(s) whose name(s) is are subscribed to the within instrument and acknowledged to me that he/she/they executed the same in his/her/their authorized capacity(ies), and that by his/her/their signature(s) on the instrument the person(s), or the entity upon behalf of which the person(s) acted, executed the instrument.

I certify under PENALTY OF PERJURY under the laws of the State of _____ that the foregoing paragraph is true and correct.

WITNESS my hand and official seal.

_____
Notary Public Signature

The following assets are hereby transferred to the Trustee as part of the Trust and will be administered and distributed in accordance with the terms of the Trust Agreement of the _____ Living Trust.

The following constitutes the property of the Settlor, and the Settlor hereby declares that all property in which the Settlor has an interest, or in which stands in the name of Settlor, is wholly the property of the Settlor under state laws, irrespective of the manner in which record title is held or has been held prior to the transfer to the Trustee under this Trust:

Bank Accounts *(Individual)*

All of the Settlor's right, title and interest in and to any bank accounts, savings and loans, or other financial institution, whether checking, savings, money markets, certificates of deposit, safe deposit boxes, or other type of account, as described herein;

Name of Bank _____

Mailing Address _____

City _____ State _____ Zip _____ Country _____

Work +___ (_____) _____ - _____ Fax +___ (_____) _____ - _____

Account Number _____

Account Number _____

Name of Bank _____

Mailing Address _____

City _____ State _____ Zip _____ Country _____

Work +___ (_____) _____ - _____ Fax +___ (_____) _____ - _____

Account Number _____

Account Number _____

Business Interests
(If Necessary, Use Multiple Pages)

All of the Settlor's beneficial interest in and to the following described business interests;

Business Name _____

Business Purpose What does the business do? _____

Structure   Other _____

Ownership   Number of Shares _____ Ownership _____%

                Number of Certificates _____ Ownership _____%

Positions   President _____

               Secretary _____

               Treasurer _____

               Director _____

Estimated Business Value   Currency _____ Amount _____

Salary or other Compensation Currency _____ Amount _____

Pensions and Profit Sharing   Currency _____ Amount _____

Gross Annual Income   Currency _____ Amount _____

Other _____   Currency _____ Amount _____

Name of Bank_____

Mailing Address _____

City _____ State _____ Zip _____ Country _____

Work +___ (_____) _____ - _____ Fax +___ (_____) _____ - _____

Account Number _____

Account Number _____

Financial Interests

All of the Settlor's right, title and interest in and to any stocks, bonds, mutual funds, Individual Retirement Accounts (IRA), 401(k), Annuities, Simplified Employment Pension Plan (SEP), or other type of financial interest, as described herein;

Name of Financial Institution _____

Mailing Address _____

City _____ State _____ Zip _____ Country _____

Work +___ (_____) _____ - _____ Fax +___ (_____) _____ - _____

Account Number _____

Account Number _____

Name of Financial Institution _____

Mailing Address _____

City _____ State _____ Zip _____ Country _____

Work +___ (_____) _____ - _____ Fax +___ (_____) _____ - _____

Account Number _____

Account Number _____

Name of Financial Institution _____

Mailing Address _____

City _____ State _____ Zip _____ Country _____

Work +___ (_____) _____ - _____ Fax +___ (_____) _____ - _____

Account Number _____

Account Number _____

Insurance

The Settlor's beneficial interest in and to the following described insurance policies;

Name of Insurance Company _____

Mailing Address _____

City _____ State _____ Zip _____ Country _____

Work +___ (_____) _____ - _____ Fax +___ (_____) _____ - _____

Policy Number_____

Policy Number_____

Name of Insurance Company _____

Mailing Address _____

City _____ State _____ Zip _____ Country _____

Work +___ (_____) _____ - _____ Fax +___ (_____) _____ - _____

Policy Number_____

Policy Number_____

Name of Insurance Company _____

Mailing Address _____

City _____ State _____ Zip _____ Country _____

Work +___ (_____) _____ - _____ Fax +___ (_____) _____ - _____

Policy Number_____

Policy Number_____

Motor Vehicles

The Settlor's beneficial interest in and to the following described cars, planes, yachts, and other types of motor vehicles;

Manufacturer _____

Model _____

Year _____

Vehicle Identification Number (VIN) _____

Additional Information _____

_____

Manufacturer _____

Model _____

Year _____

Vehicle Identification Number (VIN) _____

Additional Information _____

_____

Manufacturer _____

Model _____

Year _____

Vehicle Identification Number (VIN) _____

Additional Information _____

_____

Offshore Interests

All of the Settlor's right, title and interest in and to the following offshore business interests and the Settlor's beneficial interest in and to the following offshore financial interests;

Business Name _____

Business Purpose What does the business do? _____

Structure   Other _____

Ownership   Number of Shares _____ Ownership _____%

                       Number of Certificates _____ Ownership _____%

Positions   President   _____

                       Secretary   _____

                       Treasurer   _____

                       Director   _____

Estimated Business Value   Currency _____ Amount _____

Salary or other Compensation   Currency _____ Amount _____

Pensions and Profit Sharing   Currency _____ Amount _____

Gross Annual Income   Currency _____ Amount _____

Other _____   Currency _____ Amount _____

Name of Bank _____

Mailing Address _____

City _____ State _____ Zip _____ Country _____

Work +___ (_____) _____ - _____ Fax +___ (_____) _____ - _____

Account Number _____

Account Number _____

Personal Property

All of the Settlor's right, title and interest in and to, but not limited to, the following personal property as described herein;

antiques, bullion, china, collections and objects of art, currency and stamps, furniture and furnishings, household goods, investment or collectible coins, jewelry, personal effects, silverware, sporting equipment, wearing apparel; and

_____

_____
_____
_____
_____
_____
_____
_____
_____
_____
_____
_____
_____
_____
_____
_____
_____
_____

Real Property

All of the Settlor's right, title and interest in and to any real property, securitized notes and deeds of trust, as described herein;

Description of Real Property_____

Physical Address _____

City _____ State _____ Zip _____ Country _____

Assessor's Parcel Number _____

Additional Information _____

_____

Description of Real Property_____

Physical Address _____

City _____ State _____ Zip _____ Country _____

Assessor's Parcel Number _____

Additional Information _____

_____

Description of Real Property _____

Physical Address_____

City _____ State _____ Zip _____ Country _____

Assessor's Parcel Number _____

Additional Information _____

_____

STATEMENT AND SIGNATURE OF WITNESSES

This Statement and Signature of Witnesses is an attachment to the following document only:

_____

WE the undersigned witnesses declare under penalty of perjury that we are not related to the principal by blood, marriage, or adoption, and to the best of our knowledge, upon the principal's death, we are not entitled to any part of the principal's estate, and further that the principal is personally known to us, that the principal, is eighteen (18) years of age or older, and appeared to be of sound mind and under no duress, fraud, or undue influence and that the principal did sign the foregoing document in our presence.

Executed this _____ day of _____, 20_____

Witness #1   Signature: _____

                     Full Legal Name: _____

                     Physical Address: _____

                                        _____

                     City _____ State _____

                     Country _____ Zip _____

Witness #2   Signature: _____

                     Full Legal Name: _____

                     Physical Address: _____

                                        _____

                     City _____ State _____

                     Country _____ Zip _____

SCHEDULE "A"
TO
_____ **LIVING TRUST**

DECLARATION

The undersigned Settlor and Trustee hereby certify to have read the Schedule "A" and agree such Schedule "A" fully and accurately sets out the assets which are to fund the _____ Living Trust, and hereby approve, ratify and confirm the Schedule "A".

Executed this _____ day of _____, 20_____

_____
Settlor

_____
Settlor

NOTARY ACKNOWLEDGEMENT

STATE OF _____)

) SS.

COUNTY OF _____)

On _____ before me, _____

                                             (insert name and title of the officer)

personally appeared _____, who proved to me on the basis of satisfactory evidence to be the person(s) whose name(s) is are subscribed to the within instrument and acknowledged to me that he/she/they executed the same in his/her/ their authorized capacity(ies), and that by his/her/their signature(s) on the instrument the person(s), or the entity upon behalf of which the person(s) acted, executed the instrument.

I certify under PENALTY OF PERJURY under the laws of the State of _____ that the foregoing paragraph is true and correct.

WITNESS my hand and official seal.

_____
Notary Public Signature

www.ingramcontent.com/pod-product-compliance
Lightning Source LLC
Chambersburg PA
CBHW050834220326

41598CB00006B/364